中国思想文化术语多语种对外翻译
标准化建设项目成果

CHINESE THINKING AND CULTURE
MULTILINGUAL TERMINOLOGY DATABASE

中华源·河南故事
CHINESE CIVILIZATION
Stories from Henan

空中丝绸之路
SILK ROAD IN THE AIR

河南省人民政府外事办公室　编

河南大学出版社
HENAN UNIVERSITY PRESS
·郑州·

图书在版编目（CIP）数据

中华源·河南故事. 空中丝绸之路：汉、英 / 河南省人民政府外事办公室编. -- 郑州：河南大学出版社，2021.4

ISBN 978-7-5649-4612-8

Ⅰ. ①中… Ⅱ. ①河… Ⅲ. ①地方文化-河南-通俗读物-汉、英②航空运输-货物运输-河南-通俗读物-汉、英 Ⅳ. ① G127.61-49 ② F562.861-49

中国版本图书馆 CIP 数据核字（2021）第 062942 号

责任编辑	田丽贞
责任校对	林方丽
封面设计	翟淼淼
出版发行	河南大学出版社
	地址：郑州市郑东新区商务外环中华大厦2401号　邮编：450046
	电话：0371-86059701（营销部）
	0371-86059750（高等教育与职业教育分公司）
	网址：hupress.henu.edu.cn
排　　版	河南大学出版社设计排版部
印　　刷	河南博雅彩印有限公司
版　　次	2021年4月第1版　　印　次　2021年4月第1次印刷
开　　本	710 mm×1010 mm　1/16　　印　张　9.75
字　　数	156千　　　　　　　　　　定　价　46.00元

版权所有，侵权必究
本书如有印装质量问题，请与河南大学出版社营销部联系调换。

"中华源·河南故事"系列丛书编委会

顾　　问	黄友义　杨　平　范大祺
名誉主任	穆为民　何金平　刘炯天
主　　任	付　静
副 主 任	陈　岩　陈志伟　刁玉华　方启雄　介晓磊
	孔留安　李冰冰　李向前　李　镇　梁留科
	刘金锋　牛卫国　屈鹏飞　史永庆　田　凯
	万正峰　王建修　王清义　王自文　许二平
	杨建伟　杨玮斌　张改平　张俊峰　张明超
	张松文　赵卫东

主　　编　付　静
副 主 编　李冰冰
编　　委　陈　玮　丁　锐　高　阳　徐恒振　郑延保

中华源·河南故事·空中丝绸之路

主　　编　张明超
副 主 编　刘建葆　李　育（英文）
中文撰稿　赵　磊　崔　崑　许维鸿　白　桦　范　勇
英文译者　孙建华　韩　芳　靳　琼
英文审校　〔澳大利亚〕Robert Ashby

The Editorial Committee
Chinese Civilization
Stories from Henan

Consultants	Huang Youyi Yang Ping Fan Daqi
Honorary Directors	Mu Weimin He Jinping Liu Jiongtian
Director	Fu Jing
Deputy Directors	Chen Yan Chen Zhiwei Diao Yuhua Fang Qixiong
	Jie Xiaolei Kong Liu'an Li Bingbing Li Xiangqian
	Li Zhen Liang Liuke Liu Jinfeng Niu Weiguo
	Qu Pengfei Shi Yongqing Tian Kai Wan Zhengfeng
	Wang Jianxiu Wang Qingyi Wang Ziwen Xu Erping
	Yang Jianwei Yang Weibin Zhang Gaiping
	Zhang Junfeng Zhang Mingchao Zhang Songwen
	Zhao Weidong
Chief Editor	Fu Jing
Deputy Chief Editor	Li Bingbing
Editors	Chen Wei Ding Rui Gao Yang Xu Hengzhen
	Zheng Yanbao

Chinese Civilization
Stories from Henan
Silk Road in the Air

Editor-in-Chief	Zhang Mingchao
Associate Editors-in-Chief	Liu Jianbao Li Yu (English Text)
Writers	Zhao Lei Cui Kun Xu Weihong
	Bai Hua Fan Yong
Translators	Sun Jianhua Han Fang Jin Qiong
Translation Proofreader	Robert Ashby (A.U.)

总　序

中国是世界四大文明古国之一，也是世界上唯一的古代文明传统未曾中断的国家。河南省地处中国中东部，是中华文明和中华民族的重要发祥地，在中国五千年的文明史上，河南作为国家政治、经济、文化的中心就长达三千多年。从某种意义上讲，一部河南史就是半部中国史。这里是中华人文始祖黄帝的故乡，是古丝绸之路的东方起点，是少林功夫和陈氏太极的发源地，这里创建了中国历史上最早的都城，镌刻了中国最古老的文字，诞生了中国最初的商业文明。

伴随着新时代的荣光，河南经济社会发展迅速，人民生活水平显著提升，这是河南人民自力更生、艰苦奋斗的历史结果，也是对外开放带来的益处。河南经济社会的发展、人民生活方式的改变都植根于深层次的文化积淀。为了让世界更多地了解河南，让河南更好地走向世界，2018年以来，河南省人民政府外事办公室认真研析了这片古老土地上的历史文化资源和时代风貌，组织各领域权威专家学者，编译了"中华源·河南故事"中外文系列丛书，选取黄河文化、河洛文化、老子、庄子、黄帝、少林功夫、太极拳、中医、汉字、丝绸之路、古都、农业、大运河、文物、陶瓷、青铜器、手工艺、书法、杂技、豫菜、豫剧、脱贫攻坚、空中丝绸之路、航空城、南水北调、中国粮谷、红旗渠、焦裕禄等多个主题，力图以故事的方式向世界展现一个立体、全面、真实的河南。

当今世界，人类文明无论是在物质还是在精神方面都取得了巨大进步，特别是物质的极大丰富，这在古代世界是完全不能想象的。同时，当代人类也面临着许多突出的难题，比如，贫富差距持续扩大，物欲追求奢华无度，个人主义恶性膨胀，社会诚信不断消减，伦理道德每况愈下，人与自然关系日趋紧张，等等。要解决这些难题，不仅需要运用人类今天的智慧和力量，而且需要运用人类历史上积累和储存的智慧和力量。河南历史文化底蕴深厚、包容性强，在今天仍极具现实意义。中原文化蕴含的思想智慧有助于修身养性，推动人类社会进步发展，焦裕禄精神、红旗渠精神所体现的为民爱民、艰苦奋斗的价值取向是构建人类命运共同体的力量源泉。我们期待与读者们一起从河南故事中汲取更多的智慧和力量，共同创造更加美好的未来。

Series Foreword

China is one of the four ancient civilizations in the world, and is also the only country in the world where the ancient civilization has not been interrupted. Located in east-central China, Henan Province is an important cradle for the Chinese nation and Chinese civilization. In the course of the five thousand years of Chinese history, for more than three thousand years it served as the political, economic and cultural center of the country and therefore, as generally accepted, represents half of the history of China. Henan is the native place of Yellow Emperor, the cradle of Chinese culture, the starting point of the ancient Silk Road in the east, and the birthplace of Shaolin Kungfu and Chen-style Taijiquan—typical examples of the world-renowned Chinese martial arts. It was here that the earliest capital city in China was founded, the oldest Chinese characters engraved, and the earliest commerce took shape.

In the new era, Henan has witnessed rapid growth in its economy and remarkable improvement of people's living conditions owing to the national reform and opening-up policy and unremitting endeavors of the people. Modern economic achievements and social development as well as the changes of way of life could be traced back to its traditional values and cultural heritages. To enable people from other countries to understand Henan, and let the Province integrate more efficiently into the world development, the Foreign Affairs Office of the People's Government of Henan Province has organized teams of authoritative experts and scholars in relevant fields to compile this *Chinese Civilization: Stories from Henan* in Chinese and foreign languages since 2018 by crystallizing the excellence of traditions and outstanding features of modern development. The book series include *The Yellow River Culture*, *Heluo Culture*, *Laozi*, *Zhuangzi*, *The Yellow Emperor*, *Shaolin Kungfu*, *Taijiquan*, *Traditional Chinese Medicine*,

Chinese Characters, *The Silk Road*, *Ancient Chinese Capitals*, *Feeding the People—Agriculture*, *The Grand Canal*, *Cultural Heritage*, *Ceramic*, *Bronze*, *Handicraft Art*, *Calligraphy*, *Acrobatics*, *Henan Cuisine*, *Henan Opera*, *Poverty Alleviation*, *Silk Road in the Air*, *Zhengzhou—An Aviation City*, *South-to-North Water Diversion*, *China Grain Valley*, *Man-Made River—Hongqiqu Canal*, *A Model Official—Jiao Yulu*, etc., presenting a panoramic picture of the Province.

In today's world, human civilization has made great progress in both material accumulation and ethical advancement, and the great abundance of materials today, especially, is beyond the imagination of the ancient people. At the same time, however, modern people are also confronted with a lot of problems, such as the widening gap between the rich and the poor, the indulgence in pursuit of luxury and extravagance, the undesirable extension of individualism, the decline of social integrity, and the increasingly tense relationship between man and nature. To solve the problems, we need to draw on the wisdom and powers developed today as well as those accumulated in the past. Henan is endowed with rich historical and cultural heritages characterized by its inclusiveness, and such heritages remain significant today. The intelligence and wisdom in Henan culture are conducive to self-cultivation and to the promotion of social development. The spirit of serving the people and relentless struggle, as embodied in Jiao Yulu and Man-Made River—Hongqiqu Canal provides source of strength for building a community with a shared future for mankind. It is our hope that wisdom and strength from Henan stories could lead us to a shared brilliant future.

前 言

　　河南是中华民族和华夏文明的重要发祥地。在5000多年的中华文明史上，河南作为政治中心、经济中心、文化中心的历史就长达3000多年。河南地处中国腹地，占据承东启西、连南贯北、维系八方的枢纽地位。古往今来，河南在中国与世界的交往中始终扮演着重要的角色。

　　时光荏苒，21世纪初，河南凭借一条"天路"与世界再次实现了密切的沟通交流。2013年9月和10月，中国领导人和中国政府先后提出共建"丝绸之路经济带"和"21世纪海上丝绸之路"的重大倡议和发展规划。河南凭借区位优势主动融入"一带一路"建设，向天寻路。2013年，郑州航空港经济综合实验区发展规划得到国务院正式批复。2014年，河南民航发展投资有限公司（简称"河南航投"）与欧洲最大的全货运航空公司卢森堡国际货运航空公司（简称"卢森堡货航"）开展资本合作，实施了"双枢纽"战略合作模式，开通了首条郑州至卢森堡全货运航线。河南"空中丝绸之路"开始飞架亚欧两大洲。而后在两国政府及企业的通力合作下，河南"空中丝绸之路"在航线网络拓展、承运规模品类等领域不断拓展，构建起"一点连三洲，一线串欧美"的国际货运版图。

　　河南"空中丝绸之路"的意义在于它不仅是一条互利各国交通运输的"商路"，还是一个聚合经贸文化发展的"平台"。2017年6月14日，在中国与卢森堡两国建交45周年之际，两国领导人对河南"空中丝绸之路"给予高度的赞赏和支持。河南"空中丝绸之路"成为"一带一路"倡议中的重要内容。以经贸往来作为基础，人文交流、文化互动越来越多地成为河南"空中丝绸之路"上的主旋律。

　　经过6年的精心营造,河南"空中丝绸之路"已经由最初的从"两点一线"到"集疏全球",正助力河南成为中国内陆地区全面对外开放的新高地、中原崛起的新引擎,正助力中国与"一带一路"沿线国家实现共享共赢。

Preface

Henan is a major birthplace of the Chinese nation and Chinese civilization. Henan has been a political, economic and cultural center of Chinese civilization for more than 3,000 years. Located in the central part of China, Henan occupies the pivotal position connecting the east with the west, the south with the north, and it is the convergent point between China's many regions. Henan has played an important historic role in the exchanges between China and the outside world.

In the early 21st century, Henan has once again expanded its communication with the world via a "heavenly road". In September and October 2013, Chinese leaders put forward major initiatives and development plans for jointly building the Silk Road Economic Belt and the 21st Century Maritime Silk Road. Henan has been making proactive contribution to the development of the Belt and Road Initiative based on its unique location. In 2013, the Development Plan of the Zhengzhou Airport Economy Zone was officially approved by the State Council. In 2014, Henan Civil Aviation Development and Investment Co. Ltd. carried out capital cooperation with Cargolux Airlines International, the largest all-cargo airline in Europe, implementing the "double hubs" strategic cooperation mode and opening the first all-cargo flight route from Zhengzhou to Luxembourg. The "Silk Road in the Air" in Henan has begun to form connections across Asia and Europe. With the cooperation of governments and enterprises across the two continents, the "Silk Road in the Air" has continuously expanded its airway network, and the scale and range of cargo, with the aim of becoming a linking point among Europe, Asia and America.

The significance of Henan's "Silk Road in the Air" is that it is not only a mutually beneficial "trade route" for the transportation of various commodities, but also a platform for the development of economy, trade and culture. On June 14, 2017, on the 45th anniversary of the establishment of diplomatic ties between

China and Luxembourg, leaders of the two nations welcomed and supported the "Silk Road in the Air" in Henan Province. The "Silk Road in the Air" has become an important part of the Belt and Road Initiative. Commodity exchanges and cultural exchanges have increasingly become the theme of the "Silk Road in the Air".

After six years of meticulous construction, the trade route has been transformed from "two points and one line" to a "concordance of resources from all over the world". It is helping China's inland areas to fully open up to the outside world and has created a new engine for the rise of the Central Plains. The "Silk Road in the Air" aims to achieve win-win results for China and the countries along the Belt and Road.

目 录　　　　　　　　　　　Contents

第一章　腾飞新时代：河南"空中丝绸之路"的缘起　　001
　　一、起势：中国统筹国内、国际两个大局的顶层设计　　002
　　二、开局：河南"空中丝绸之路"的先手落子　　012
　　三、河南"空中丝绸之路"的谋划发展　　026

Chapter 1　Soaring in the New Era: the Origin of the "Silk Road in the Air" in Henan Province　　001
　　I. China Coordinating the Top-Level Design Based on Domestic and International Situations　　003
　　II. Henan as the First Mover in the "Silk Road in the Air" Construction　　013
　　III. The Plan of the "Silk Road in the Air" in Henan Province　　027

第二章　联通跨五洲：河南"空中丝绸之路"的成效　　047
　　一、河南"空中丝绸之路"主业示范效应突出，拉动了合作双方航空运输业务实现共赢发展　　048
　　二、河南"空中丝绸之路"产业集聚效应突出，推动了河南省地方经济社会高质量发展　　060
　　三、河南"空中丝绸之路"人文交流效应突出，促进了中外旅游历史交流互动　　076
　　四、河南"空中丝绸之路"带路引领效应突出，推动了中国与西方国家、南南国家双方向关系突破　　082

Chapter 2　Connecting Five Continents: the Achievements of the "Silk Road in the Air" in Henan Province　　047
　　I. The Demonstration Effect of Henan's "Silk Road in the Air" in Promoting the Win-Win Development of the Air Transport Business　　049

II. The Agglomeration Effect of Henan's "Silk Road in the Air" in Pushing
　　Henan's Local Economy to the Level of High-quality Development　061
III. The Promotion of Tourism and Cultural Exchanges between China and
　　Foreign Countries　077
IV. The "Silk Road in the Air" in Henan has Improved Relations between China
　　and Western Countries, and between China and South-South Countries　083

第三章　寄语新未来：河南"空中丝绸之路"的趋势　087
　　一、打造"一带一路"建设的河南模式　088
　　二、最佳"一带一路"国际航空物流业合作实践　112

Chapter 3　Outlook on the Future: Trends of the "Silk Road in the Air" in
　　Henan Province　087
　　I. Henan's Contribution to the Belt and Road Initiative　089
　　II. International Aviation Logistics Cooperation under the Belt and
　　　Road Initiative　113

附：　河南"空中丝绸之路"大事记　122
Appendix: Milestones of the "Silk Road in the Air" in Henan Province　123

第一章

腾飞新时代：河南"空中丝绸之路"的缘起

Chapter 1

Soaring in the New Era: the Origin of the "Silk Road in the Air" in Henan Province

一、起势:中国统筹国内、国际两个大局的顶层设计

中国最近30多年的发展经验表明,坚持统筹国内、国际两个大局是如期实现全面建成小康社会奋斗目标、推动经济社会持续健康发展必须遵循的原则之一。"全方位对外开放是发展的必然要求。必须坚持打开国门搞建设,既立足国内,充分运用我国资源、市场、制度等优势,又重视国内、国际经济联动效应,积极应对外部环境变化,更好利用两个市场、两种资源,推动互利共赢、共同发展。"[1]

经济全球化使得各国经济相互联系、相互影响达到了前所未有的程度。如何把外部环境变化当作谋划国内发展不可忽视的变量,中国的"一带一路"倡议给出了回答。

2013年,中国国家主席习近平先后提出建设"丝绸之路经济带"和"21世纪海上丝绸之路"重大倡议,引发了越来越多国家的响应。共建"一带一路"成为中国参与全球开放合作、改善全球经济治理体系、促进全球共同发展繁荣、推动构建人类命运共同体的中国方案。

2015年,《推动共建丝绸之路经济带和21世纪海上丝绸之路的愿景与行动》正式发布,明确提出"一带一路"是一项系统工程,要坚持共商、共建、共享原则。中国将充分发挥国内各地区的比较优势,实行更加积极主动的开放战略。在内陆地区,利用内陆纵深广阔、人力资源丰富、产业基础较好的优势,依托长江中游城市群、成渝城市群、中原城市群、呼包鄂榆城市群、哈长城市群等重点区域,推动区域互动合作和产业集聚发展,打造重庆西部开发开放重要支撑和成都、郑州、武汉、长沙、南昌、合肥等内陆开放型经济高地。支持郑州、西安等内陆城市

---

[1]《中共中央关于制定国民经济和社会发展第十三个五年规划的建议》。

I. China Coordinating the Top-Level Design Based on Domestic and International Situations

China's experience in development over the past 30-plus years shows that balancing domestic and international interests is one of the principles that must be followed to complete the building of a moderately prosperous society and promote sustained and sound economic and social development. "Opening up to the outside world is necessary for development. We must continue to pursue development with an open mind. We must make full use of China's advantages in resources, market and system, and at the same time pay attention to the interconnected effects of the domestic and international economies. We must actively respond to changes in the external environment and make better use of the two markets and resources to promote mutual benefit and common development." [1]

Economic globalization has brought the economies of all countries into contact with each other to an unprecedented extent. China's Belt and Road Initiative is a response to the changing external environment, which cannot be ignored when planning domestic development.

In 2013, Chinese President Xi Jinping put forward the major initiatives of building the Silk Road Economic Belt and the 21st Century Maritime Silk Road, which have grown to incorporate more and more countries. The Belt and Road Initiative is China's plan to participate in global opening and cooperation, improve global economic governance, promote common development and prosperity, and build a shared future for mankind.

In 2015, *Vision and Actions on Jointly Building Silk Road Economic Belt and 21st-Century Maritime Silk Road to Promote the Implementation of the Initiative* was officially released, which stated that the Belt and Road Initiative is a systematic project and should be jointly built through consultation to meet the

---

[1] *Proposal of the Central Committee of the Communist Party of China on the Formulation of the Thirteenth Five-Year Plan for National Economic and Social Development*

建设航空港、国际陆港，加强内陆口岸与沿海、沿边口岸通关合作，开展跨境贸易电子商务服务试点。

2017年5月14日至15日，首届"一带一路"国际合作高峰论坛在北京举行，包括29个国家的元首和政府首脑在内，140多个国家、80多个国际组织的代表齐聚北京。高峰论坛发布了圆桌峰会联合公报，达成了270多项成果。"一带一路"开始进入国际话语体系，写入了联合国大会、安理会等重要决议。以双边合作筑底、多边机制呼应、高峰论坛引领的"三位一体"国际合作架构初步形成。

2019年4月25日至27日，第二届"一带一路"国际合作高峰论坛在北京召开。包括中国在内，38个国家的元首和政府首脑等领导人以及联合国秘书长和国际货币基金组织总裁共40位领导人出席了圆桌峰会。在高峰论坛筹备进程中和举办期间，各方达成283项具体成果，签署了总额超过640亿美元的项目合作协议。当年新增16个国家和国际组织同中国签署共建"一带一路"合作文件，使共同推进"一带一路"建设政府间合作文件总数升至199份。"携手努力让各国互联互通更加有效，经济增长更加强劲，国际合作更加密切，人民生活更加美好"成为"一带一路"的共同目标。共建"一带一路"成为推动构建人类命运共同体的重要实践平台。

2020年一季度，新冠肺炎疫情在全球范围内爆发，对各国经济社会发展造成了前所未有的冲击。"一带一路"却展现出强大活力。据中国海关总署统计，2020年第一季度，中国对"一带一路"沿线国家外贸进出口达到2.07万亿元，同比增长3.2%。中国商务部数据显示，中国企业2020年第一季度在"一带一路"沿线52个国家非金融类直接投资达42亿美元，同比增长11.7%。这充分地展示了"一带一路"倡议所体现的人类命运共同体理念的重要性，让世界重新思考国际合作的重要性。

interests of all. China will give full play to the advantages of its various regions and adopt a more proactive opening-up strategy. "In order to promote regional industrial cooperation, support development in the west of Chongqing, and reach economic heights in Chengdu, Zhengzhou, Wuhan, Changsha, Nanchang, Hefei and other inland open areas, the use of deep and abundant human resources and good industrial foundations are greatly emphasized, relying on key urban agglomerations such as those in the middle region of the Yangtze River, Chengdu and Chongqing, Harbin and Changchun, Henan, and Inner Mongolia." "We will support inland cities such as Zhengzhou and Xi'an in building airports and international land ports, strengthen customs clearance cooperation between inland ports and coastal and border ports, and pilot cross-border trade E-commerce services."

On May 14 and 15, 2017, the first Belt and Road Forum for International Cooperation was held in Beijing. Heads of 29 countries and representatives from more than 140 countries and 80 international organizations participated in the forum. A joint communique of the roundtable summit listed more than 270 outcomes. The Belt and Road Initiative has entered the international discourse system and been included in resolutions of the United Nations (UN) General Assembly and Security Council. A "three-in-one" international cooperation architecture, based on bilateral cooperation, echoed by multilateral mechanisms and led by the summit forum, has taken shape.

From April 25 to April 27, 2019, the second Belt and Road Forum for International Cooperation was held in Beijing. Leaders from 38 countries, including China, as well as the Secretary General of the UN and President of the International Monetary Fund (IMF) attended the roundtable summit. During the preparatory process and summit, the parties reached 283 concrete outcomes and signed cooperation agreements on projects totaling more than 64 billion U.S. dollars. In the same year, 16 more countries and international organizations signed cooperation documents on jointly building the Belt and Road Initiative with China, bringing the total number of intergovernmental cooperation documents on the Belt and Road Initiative to 199. "Working together to make connectivity more effective, economic growth more robust, international cooperation closer and people's lives better" has become the common goal of the Belt and Road Initiative,

> **专栏："一带一路"建设中航空领域互联互通的成效**
>
> 加快设施联通建设是共建"一带一路"的关键领域和核心内容。《共建"一带一路"倡议：进展、贡献与展望》报告表明，经过5年多时间的共同建设，在航空运输领域，中国与126个国家和地区签署了双边政府间航空运输协定，与卢森堡、俄罗斯、亚美尼亚、印度尼西亚、柬埔寨、孟加拉国、以色列、蒙古、马来西亚、埃及等国家扩大了航权安排。中国与沿线国家新增国际航线1239条，占新开通国际航线总量的69.1%。

进入21世纪，中国经济发展原有动力有所减弱，需要把进口和出口、利用外资和对外投资统筹协调起来，把全方位对外开放和国内产业转型升级、空间结构优化布局有机结合起来，从而打造出中国经济发展的新动力。

2012年，全面建成小康社会和全面深化改革开放成为指引中国发展的宏伟目标，中国未来需要实现经济建设、政治建设、文化建设、社会建设、生态文明建设"五位一体"总体布局。

2013年，《中共中央关于全面深化改革若干重大问题的决定》提出："要扩大内陆沿边开放，抓住全球产业重新布局机遇，推动内陆贸易、投资、技术创新协调发展。支持内陆城市增开国际客、货运航线，发展多式联运，形成横贯东、中、西，联结南、北方的对外经济走廊。"同年12月，中央全面深化改革领导小组正式成立，明确了要着重推进经济体制和生态文明体制等多领域改革。

2014年12月，中央经济工作会议对中国经济发展阶段做出新论断，即中国经济正在向形态更高级、分工更复杂、结构更合理的阶段演化，经济发展进入新常态。传统产业相对饱和，传统产业供给能力大幅超出需求，产业结构必须优化升级。必须让创新成为驱动发展新引擎。

which itself has become an important platform for building a shared future for mankind.

In the first quarter of 2020, the COVID-19 epidemic broke out on a global scale, causing an unprecedented impact on the economic and social development of all countries. Meanwhile, the Belt and Road Initiative continued to show great energy. According to statistics on the General Administration of Customs, in the first quarter of 2020, China's foreign trade imports and exports from countries along the Belt and Road route reached 2.07 trillion Yuan, a year-on-year increase of 3.2%. Data from China's Ministry of Commerce showed that non-financial direct investment by Chinese enterprises in 52 countries along the Belt and Road route reached 4.2 billion U.S. dollars in the first quarter, a year-on-year increase of 11.7%. It has demonstrated the importance of the concept of "a shared future for mankind" embodied in the Belt and Road Initiative, and made the world rethink the importance of international cooperation.

Column: Achievements of Aviation Connectivity under the Belt and Road Initiative

Accelerating infrastructure connectivity is the key area and core content of jointly building the Belt and Road Initiative. According to the report *Jointly Building the Belt and Road Initiative: Progress, Contribution and Prospects*, after five years of joint development, China has signed bilateral intergovernmental air transport agreements with 126 countries and regions. Navigation rights arrangements have been expanded with Luxembourg, Russia, Armenia, Indonesia, Cambodia, Bangladesh, Israel, Mongolia, Malaysia and Egypt. China and countries along the Belt and Road added 1,239 new international routes, accounting for 69.1 % of new international routes worldwide.

In the 21st century, the motive force for China's economic development has weakened, so we need to coordinate import and export, and utilize foreign capital and outbound investment. We need to combine all-round opening up with transformation and upgrading of domestic industries and the optimized layout of China's spatial structure, so as to create a new driving force for China's economic

2015年5月,《中国制造2025》正式发布,提出通过"三步走"实现制造强国的战略目标:第一步,到2025年迈入制造强国行列;第二步,到2035年整体达到世界制造强国阵营中等水平;第三步,到新中国成立100年时综合实力进入世界制造强国前列。10月,《中共中央关于制定国民经济和社会发展第十三个五年规划的建议》提出了全面建成小康社会新的目标要求。12月,中央经济工作会议提出要坚持以提高经济发展质量和效益为中心,主动适应经济发展新常态。推进供给侧结构性改革,在适度扩大总需求的同时,去产能、去库存、去杠杆、降成本、补短板,提高供给体系质量和效率,提高投资有效性,加快培育新的发

development.

In 2012, building a moderately prosperous society, while deepening reform and opening up, became the grand goals guiding China's development. In the future, China needs to realize the "Five-sphere Integrated Plan" for economic, political, cultural, social and ecological progress.

In 2013, the *Central Committee of the Communist Party of China's Decision on Some Major Issues Concerning Comprehensively Deepening Reform* stated, "We should open inland and border areas wider to the outside world, seize the opportunity of redistributing global industries, and promote coordinated development of inland trade, investment, and technological innovation. We will support inland cities in opening more international passenger and freight routes and developing multi-modal transport to form an external economic corridor that links the East, the West, the South and the North." In December of the same year, the Central Leading Group for Deepening Overall Reform was formally established, and it was made clear that economic reform and ecological progress should be promoted.

In December 2014, the Central Economic Work Conference made a new judgment on the state of China's economic development: The Chinese economy had evolved to a more advanced form, with more complex division of labor and a more rational structure, and economic development had entered a new normal. Traditional industries have become relatively saturated, with supply capacity greatly exceeding demand, so the industrial structure must be optimized and upgraded. Innovation must become the new engine of development.

In May 2015, *Made in China 2025* was officially released, proposing the strategic goal of achieving manufacturing power through three steps. The first step is to become a manufacturing power by 2025; the second is to reach the middle level of the world manufacturing power camp by 2035; the third is to achieve comprehensive strength as the world's foremost manufacturing power 100 years after the founding of new China. In October, the *Proposal of the Central Committee of the Communist Party of China on the Formulation of the Thirteenth Five-year Plan for National Economic and Social Development* set out new goals and requirements for completing the building of a moderately prosperous society. In December, the Central Economic Work Conference

展动能。

  2017年，中国政府提出今后五年是决胜全面建成小康社会、开启全面建设社会主义现代化新征程的关键时期。"全面深化改革"成为新时代坚持和发展中国特色社会主义的基本方略，提高供给体系质量作为主攻方向。在建设现代化经济体系、建设创新型国家等多领域内，提出了158项改革举措。中国经济发展进入了新时代，由高速增长阶段转入高质量发展阶段。

nominated improving the quality and efficiency of economic development as the central task. China needs to advance supply-side structural reform, appropriately expand aggregate demand, cut overcapacity, reduce inventories, deleverage, reduce costs, and strengthen weak links. We will improve the quality and efficiency of the supply system, increase the effectiveness of investment, and foster new growth drivers at a faster pace.

In 2017, the Chinese Government identified the next five years as a crucial period for building of a moderately prosperous society and embarking on a new journey of all-round socialist modernization. "Comprehensively deepening reform" has become the basic strategy for developing socialism with Chinese characteristics in the new era, with improving the quality of the supply system as the main focus. In building a modern and innovative economy, 158 reform measures were put forward. China's economy has entered a new era, moving from a stage of rapid growth to a stage of high-quality development.

二、开局：河南"空中丝绸之路"的先手落子

河南地处"中国之中"，交通网络发达，具有发展航空物流的先天优势。长期以来，河南为探索内陆地区对外开放的战略突破口，重视航空产业以及航空经济的发展。2007年，河南省委、省政府提出了民航优先发展战略。2011年，河南省全面启动了郑州国内大型航空枢纽建设。2013年，郑州航空港经济综合实验区作为中国首个国家级航空港经济综合实验区正式开始运作，开辟国际航线、优先发展航空货运成为河南的重点工作之一。经过多年发展，河南的航空及相关行业的产业发展布局、空间基础格局以及政策支持环境日渐完善。

2013年，河南铺就"空中丝绸之路"的机遇在万里之外的欧洲国家——卢森堡出现了。为满足欧盟法律关于公平竞争的相关规定，卢森堡政府决定于2013年初正式对外出售卢森堡国际货运航空公司（简称"卢森堡货航"）的股权。作为省属航空经济投融资平台，河南民航发展投资有限公司（简称"河南航投"）及时抓住难得的机遇，开始落子布局搭建河南"空中丝绸之路"。

河南与卢森堡两地虽然相距遥远，但是优势互补、战略契合的吸引力消除了空间隔离。

河南具有与卢森堡相似的地缘优势，是中国陆路交通的重要交汇点，是中国首个航空港经济综合实验区的所在地，具有强大的空间影响力。得益于前期已完成的布局与建设，河南的航空业以及航空经济具备了良好的发展基础和外部环境。参与双方合作的主导企业在民航运输、航空物流、金融投资、通用航空、航空制造等产业板块，具有高效务实的合作态度、融合共赢的企业文化。如果能成功收购卢森堡货航的股权，那么中方企业今后在协调公司国际航班时刻资源、航权和航线资源、地面配套资源等方面都将拥有重要的话语权，与外方之间也将由以

II. Henan as the First Mover in the "Silk Road in the Air" Construction

Henan is located in the middle of China, whose transportation network is developed, and is well-situated for developing aviation logistics. For a long time, Henan has paid attention to the development of the aviation industry and the aviation economy in order to explore the strategic benefits of opening the inland to the outside world. In 2007, Henan's Provincial Party Committee and the Provincial Government put forward the civil aviation priority development strategy. In 2011, Henan Province launched the construction of a large-scale domestic aviation hub in Zhengzhou. In 2013, the Zhengzhou Airport Economic Zone—the first state-level experimental economic area of this type in China—was officially put into operation. It has become one of Henan's key tasks to open up international routes and to give priority to the development of air cargo. After years of development, Henan's aviation and related industries have gradually improved their industrial deployment for development, setup of infrastructural space and policy support environment.

In 2013, Henan's opportunity to build an "Silk Road in the Air" appeared in Luxembourg, a European country thousands of miles away. In order to meet the requirements of European Union laws on fair competition, the Luxembourg government decided to officially sell its stock in Cargolux Airlines International at the beginning of 2013. As a provincial aviation economic investment and financing platform, Henan Civil Aviation Development and Investment Co., Ltd. promptly seized the rare opportunity and began to build the "Silk Road in the Air" in Henan.

Although Henan and Luxembourg are far away from each other, their complementary advantages and strategic compatibility eliminate the distance.

Henan is an important intersection of China's land transportation, and the location of China's first Airport Economy Zone, giving it geographical influence and advantages similar to Luxembourg. Thanks to the successful completion of early stage planning and construction, Henan's aviation industry has a good foundation for development. The enterprises participating in bilateral cooperation

往松散的、缺乏约束力的单纯业务合作伙伴转变为可以设计主导"空中丝绸之路"发展的深度战略发展同盟。

卢森堡是欧洲的心脏，是全球第二大、欧洲最大的基金管理中心。作为欧洲最大的定期货运航空公司，卢森堡货航拥有行业内最为先进的货运机队，是首家同时配备两种飞机类型的运营商，拥有现代化的波音747-400和波音747-8F货机机队，拥有覆盖全球的航线网络和市场资源、完善的航空物流系统和丰富的航空货运经验，同时，拥有一系列质量控制、高价值货物运输、危险品运输、冷链运输等国际资质认证，并具有独立的飞机维修能力及完善的飞行员培训体系。

2013年初，河南省政府和河南航投先后与卢森堡有关政府机构和公司进行洽谈，表达了收购卢森堡货航35%股权的意愿，并且提出了相关商业合作计划。从4月开始，河南省政府部门以及相关企业与卢森堡方开展了多轮沟通谈判。6月，河南航投正式进入卢森堡货航股权出售的竞标程序。9月29日，中—卢双方谈判团队就合作的有关法律文本进行了讨论，达成了基本合作意向。而后又经过多轮接触磋商，11月28日，卢森堡政府正式宣布河南航投在并购竞标中胜出，同意河南航投出资2.1625亿美元收购卢森堡货航35%的股权。

2014年1月14日，河南航投收购卢森堡货航股权暨双方商业合作签约仪式在郑州举行。卢森堡货航正式落户郑州航空港经济综合实验区。

在合作初期，河南航投与卢森堡货航就经济发展战略进行了交流沟通，研究确定要打造郑州—卢森堡"空中丝绸之路"，构建以郑州为亚太物流中心、以卢森堡为欧美物流中心的"双枢纽"发展战略。

2014年4月23日，中—卢双方完成了股权交割。5月1日，来自卢森堡、法国、德国和意大利4个国家的葡萄酒、啤酒及奶制品三大类共25个品种的货物由卢森堡货航的飞机运抵郑州，总重45吨。6月27日，满载欧洲商品的波音747-8F全货机"郑州号"降落在郑州新郑国际机场，随后它满载中国的货物从郑州直飞卢森堡芬德尔机场。"郑州号"的一

have achieved mutually advantageous results in the sectors of civil aviation transportation, aviation logistics, financial investment, general aviation, aviation manufacturing and other industries. Purchasing equity stock in Cargolux Airlines International will strengthen Chinese enterprises' power and influence in the international coordination of the company in terms of flight schedules, navigation, aviation rights, airline resources and on-the-ground supporting resources. Thanks to the "Silk Road in the Air" Initiative, the relationship between the parties will develop from a loose partnership to a strategic alliance.

Luxembourg is the heart of Europe, being the largest fund management center in Europe, and the second largest in the world. As the largest scheduled cargo airline in Europe, Cargolux Airlines International has the most advanced cargo fleet in the industry. It was the first operator to be equipped with two aircraft types at the same time. It has a modern fleet of Boeing 747-400 and Boeing 747-8F freighters. It has a global network and market resources, an extensive aviation logistics system and rich air freight experience. It has the highest standards of quality control, is equipped to deal with high value cargo transportation, transportation of dangerous goods and cold chain transportation, and has independent aircraft maintenance capacity, an exceptional pilot training system, and numerous other international qualifications.

At the beginning of 2013, the Government of Henan Province and Henan Civil Aviation Development and Investment Co., Ltd. held talks with relevant government agencies and companies in Luxembourg, expressing their willingness to acquire 35% of the shares of its airlines and proposing relevant business cooperation plans. Since April, the governmental departments of Henan Province and relevant enterprises have held several rounds of communication and negotiation with Cargolux Airlines International. In June, Henan Civil Aviation Development and Investment Co., Ltd. formally entered the bidding process for the share sale of Cargolux Airlines International. On September 29, the negotiating teams of China and Luxembourg discussed the relevant legal texts for cooperation and reached the basic intention of cooperation. After several rounds of contacts and consultations, on November 28, the Government of Luxembourg officially announced that Henan Civil Aviation Development and Investment Co., Ltd. had won the acquisition bid, and agreed that Henan Civil Aviation

来一去，标志着郑州—卢森堡中欧"双枢纽"战略进入实质性运营阶段，卢森堡货航成为入驻郑州新郑国际机场的首个国际货运航空基地公司。河南"空中丝绸之路"开始横贯中欧。

专栏：我们为什么选择河南？——卢森堡货航董事会主席保罗·海明格谈"空中丝绸之路"

2014年6月27日，当郑州—卢森堡"空中丝绸之路"开通时，卢森堡货航董事会主席保罗·海明格随"郑州号"飞抵郑州。在接受采访时，他解释了卢森堡货航之所以在众多的竞争者中选择河南、选择郑州的原因：

"我们一直希望加大对中国市场的开拓力度，但没有找到合适的机会。郑州航空港经济综合实验区的建设，为航空货运企业提供了良好的业务发展机会和发展平台。"

Development and Investment Co., Ltd. would buy 35% of the shares of Cargolux Airlines International for 216.25 million U.S. dollars.

On January 14, 2014, the signing ceremony of Henan Civil Aviation Development and Investment Co., Ltd. acquiring the equity of Cargolux Airlines International and the bilateral business cooperation was held in Zhengzhou. Cargolux Airlines International officially settled in Zhengzhou Airport Economic Zone.

At the beginning of the cooperation, Henan Civil Aviation Development and Investment Co., Ltd. and Cargolux Airlines International communicated on the economic development strategy for the airline, determining to build a Zhengzhou-Luxembourg "Silk Road in the Air" with Zhengzhou as the logistics center in the Asia-Pacific region and Luxembourg as the logistics center in Europe and America.

On April 23, 2014, China and Luxembourg completed the equity delivery. On May 1, cargo weighing 45 tons, including 25 kinds of wine, beer and dairy products from Luxembourg, France, Germany and Italy arrived in Zhengzhou on the flight of Cargolux Airlines International. On June 27, the Boeing 747-8F freighter, named Zhengzhou, loaded with European goods, landed at Zhengzhou Xinzheng International Airport and returned to Findel International Airport in Luxembourg with products from China. The round trip marked the Zhengzhou-Luxembourg "double hubs" strategy entering the substantive operation stage. Cargolux Airlines International became the first international air freight company to enter Zhengzhou Xinzheng International Airport. The "Silk Road in the Air" in Henan Province has begun its journey across China and Europe.

Column: Why Did We Choose Henan? The Opinion of Paul Hemminge, Chairman of the Board of Directors of Cargolux Airlines International, on the "Silk Road in the Air"

On June 27, 2014, when the "Silk Road in the Air" between Zhengzhou and Luxembourg was opened, the chairman of the board of directors of Cargolux Airlines International, Paul Hemminge, flew to Zhengzhou with freighter "Zhengzhou". In an interview, he explained why Cargolux Airlines

> "最终选择河南,是因为政府没有把一条航线仅仅当成一个交易,而是当作一个地区发展航空经济的突破口。亚太地区是航空业发展最具潜力的市场,尤其是中国。河南拥有优越的地理位置,是连接卢森堡与欧美国家的完美纽带。从商业的角度来说,通过郑州机场这个门户打开亚太地区巨大的航空市场,也是符合客观规律的。"
>
> ——《河南日报》2014年6月30日

河南"空中丝绸之路"起步是铿锵有力的。在航线开通后短短5个月内,河南"空中丝绸之路"展现出多层面的成效。

航线运力快速增长。郑州—卢森堡航线每班进口运量从最初的57吨升至最高的104吨,每班出口运量从106吨升至最高的127吨。2014年11月23日,来自卢森堡芬德尔机场的波音747–8F全货机"郑州号"第62次抵达郑州,河南"空中丝绸之路"郑州—卢森堡国际航线在通航后短短5个月内货运量突破了10 000吨。该运量占郑州新郑国际机场同期货运增量的23.4%,占机场同期国际货运增量的29.3%。

航线流速加速发展。在开通初期,郑州—卢森堡航线每周运营2班;9月4日,航线加密至每周3班;10月15日,航线加密至每周4班;11月25日,航线加密至每周5班。

货物种类日渐丰富。最初航线货运品种单一,而后迅速增至九大类百余个品种,其中既包括羊毛制品、纺织品、玩具等传统轻工业产品,也有笔记本电脑、通讯设备、手机等电子产品,还有动车组件、汽车配件、马达轴等科技含量高的装备制造业产品。

空间辐射范围扩大。在中国地区,航班出发地和目的地覆盖除河南全省外,还辐射影响到北京、上海、天津、吉林、辽宁、山东、山西、陕西、湖北、浙江、江苏、福建、广州以及香港、台湾等15个省市地

International chose Henan and Zhengzhou among many competitors:

"We have been looking to increase our exposure to the Chinese market but have not found the right opportunity. The construction of the Zhengzhou Airport Economic Zone provides a good business development opportunity and development platform for air cargo enterprises."

"In the end, Henan was chosen because the government did not treat a route as just a transaction, but as a breakthrough for a region to develop its aviation economy. The Asia-Pacific region is the most promising market for aviation development, especially China. Henan, with a superior geographical location, is the perfect link between Luxembourg and the European and American countries. From a business point of view, it is also in line with the objective law to open the huge aviation market in the Asia-Pacific region through the gateway of Zhengzhou Airport."

— *Henan Daily*, June 30, 2014

The start of the "Silk Road in the Air" in Henan has been steady and powerful. Within five months of its launch, the "Silk Road in the Air" in Henan Province achieved multifaceted results.

Airline capacity in Zhengzhou grew rapidly. The Zhengzhou-Luxembourg route saw imports rise from an initial 57 tons to a peak of 104 tons per flight, and exports rise from 106 tons to a peak of 127 tons per flight. On November 23, 2014, the Boeing 747-8F freighter "Zhengzhou" from Luxembourg's Fincel Airport arrived in Zhengzhou for the 62nd time, with the cargo volume of the Zhengzhou-Luxembourg international route exceeding 10,000 tons in just five months after its opening. This volume accounted for 23.4% of the freight increase and 29.3% of the international freight increase of Zhengzhou Xinzheng International Airport in the same period.

The opening of air freight lanes in Zhengzhou is accelerating. During the initial period of operation, Zhengzhou-Luxembourg airlines opened 2 flights per week. On September 4, the number of flights was increased to 3 per week; on October 15, 4 per week; and on November 25, 5 flights per week.

The air cargo is comprised of an increasing variety of goods, including

区。在欧洲地区，航班出发地和目的地覆盖到德国、英国、法国、意大利、芬兰、比利时等欧洲国家以及中欧大部分地区的广阔市场。

快速起步的河南"空中丝绸之路"为中国"一带一路"建设发挥出积极的助推作用。2015年1月6日，卢森堡首相格扎维埃·贝泰尔在接受新华社记者采访时表示，卢森堡货航与河南航投开展合作一年多来取得的丰硕成果表明，中国"丝绸之路经济带"和"21世纪海上丝绸之路"战略构想为中国和世界创造了共赢机遇。"中国强，则欧洲强；中国弱，则欧洲和中国可能陷入双败局面。欧洲与中国互存互补，应在彼此

traditional light industrial products such as wool products, textiles, toys, etc., and laptops, communication equipment, mobile phones and other electronic products, as well as fast train components, auto parts, motor shafts and other high technology equipment.

The geographical coverage of Zhengzhou's "Silk Road in the Air" has expanded. In China, flights cover 15 provinces and regions, including Beijing, Shanghai, Tianjin, Jilin, Liaoning, Shandong, Shanxi, Shaanxi, Hubei, Zhejiang, Jiangsu, Fujian, Guangzhou, Hong Kong and Taiwan. In Europe, flights cover a vast market in Germany, the United Kingdom, France, Italy, Finland, Belgium and other European countries, as well as most parts of central Europe.

The rapidly developed "Silk Road in the Air" in Henan Province has played an active role in boosting China's "Belt and Road" Initiative. On January 6, 2015, Luxembourg's Prime Minister, Xavier Bettel said in an interview with Xinhua News Agency that "more than a year of fruitful results of the cooperation between Cargolux Airlines International and Henan Civil Aviation Development and Investment Co., Ltd. show that China's Silk Road Economic Belt and the 21st Century Maritime Silk Road create win-win opportunities for China and the world." "When China is strong, Europe is strong; if China is weak, Europe and China could be in a lose-lose situation. Europe and China are complementary to each other and should, on the basis of mutual respect, make full use of each other's advantages and learn from each other for common development."

Cooperation between the Chinese and Luxembourg Governments and enterprises has also become closer thanks to the "Silk Road in the Air". In January 2015, the National Civil Aviation Administration of China signed a memorandum of understanding on air transport cooperation with the Ministry of Sustainable Development and Basic Industries of Luxembourg. Henan Civil Aviation Development and Investment Co., Ltd. signed a memorandum of cooperation with Cargolux Airlines International.

The foundation of the "Silk Road in the Air" in the field of air transport has led to the upgrading of trade cooperation between China and Luxembourg. On January 23, 2015, Cross-border E-trade of Henan Civil Aviation Development and Investment Co., Ltd. and the "Fresh Luxembourg" Project was officially launched in the Zhengzhou Airport Economic Zone. This signifies that the

尊重的基础上，充分利用各自优势，相互借鉴，共同发展。"

中—卢政府以及企业层面的合作也因河南"空中丝绸之路"而变得更为密切。2015年1月，中国民用航空局与卢森堡可持续发展与基础产业部签署了航空运输合作谅解备忘录。河南航投与卢森堡货航签署了合作备忘录。

河南"空中丝绸之路"在航空运输领域的稳步开局，带动了中—卢双方在贸易合作领域随之升级。2015年1月23日，河南航投跨境E贸易暨"新鲜卢森堡"项目在郑州航空港经济综合实验区正式启动。这突破了双方原有的航空运输行业合作，标志着河南"空中丝绸之路"上的合作已经由航空运输拓展至国际贸易，标志着河南"空中丝绸之路"由郑州—卢森堡"双枢纽"向买卖全球目标的迈进。

为实现买卖全球的目标，河南"空中丝绸之路"需要建立起能覆盖全球的航空运输网络。2015年，河南"空中丝绸之路"迈出了新步伐。5月18日，卢森堡货航"郑州号"在完成卢森堡—郑州航程后再次装运货物，然后直飞美国芝加哥奥黑尔机场，开启了它的欧—亚—北美环球飞之旅。这次航程标志着卢森堡—郑州—芝加哥国际货运航线正式开通。这条国际货运航线的开通为河南民航史留下了浓墨重彩的一笔：它是郑州新郑国际机场第一条采用第五航权[1]的国际货运航线，横跨欧洲、亚洲、北美三大主要经济区域，构成了环球飞循环网络，使郑州成为联通欧洲与美洲的重要航空节点，真正实现了"一点连三洲，一线串欧美"的国际货运版图，对郑州打造全球航空枢纽具有重要的推动作用。

河南"空中丝绸之路"超预期发展态势进一步激发了中—卢双方加强合作的热情。2015年6月19日，时值郑州—卢森堡"空中丝绸之路"

---

[1] 第五航权即第三国运输权。市场准入权授权国允许承运人的定期国际航班在授权国装载来自第三国的客、货，或从授权国装载客、货飞往第三国。

cooperation on Henan's "Silk Road in the Air" has expanded from aviation transport to the international trade, and that Henan's "Silk Road in the Air" has become an international hub of buying and selling.

In order to achieve the goal of facilitating global trade, Henan's "Silk Road in the Air" needs to establish an air transport network that can cover the whole world. In 2015, new steps were taken to expand the "Silk Road in the Air". On May 18, the international cargo airline freighter "Zhengzhou", after completing its Luxembourg-Zhengzhou voyage, loaded the cargo again and then flew to Chicago O'Hare Airport in the United States, beginning its round-the-world flight, involving Europe, Asia and North America. This voyage marks the official opening of the international freight route between Luxembourg, Zhengzhou and Chicago. This international freight route is a landmark in Henan's civil aviation history. It is the first international air cargo route for Zhengzhou Xinzheng International Airport observing the Fifth Freedom [1]. The freight route covers the three major economic regions in Europe, Asia and North America. The global circulation network makes Zhengzhou an important aviation connection point between Europe and America, truly achieving the goal of connecting three continents.

The success of the "Silk Road in the Air" in Henan has further stimulated enthusiasm for cooperation between China and Luxemburg. On June 19, 2015 on the first anniversary of the opening of the "Silk Road in the Air" between Zhengzhou and Luxembourg, Henan Civil Aviation Development and Investment Co., Ltd. and Cargolux Airlines International signed two agreements on setting up a cargo airline joint venture and an aircraft maintenance company in Zhengzhou with a vision of achieving mutual trust, reciprocity and mutual benefit through deeper cooperation.

The "Silk Road in the Air" in Henan Province links Zhengzhou and Luxembourg, which are thousands of miles apart. In 2015, in order to celebrate

---

[1] The Fifth Freedom is the right of transportation of the third country. The authorized country of market access right allows the carrier's regular international flights to download or load passengers and goods from the authorized country to the third country.

开通一周年之际，河南航投与卢森堡货航就在郑州成立中国合资货运航空公司、郑州合资飞机维修公司签署了两项合作协议，期待通过更深层次的合作来实现互信、互助、互惠、互利。

河南"空中丝绸之路"将郑州和卢森堡两个相隔万里的城市联系在一起。一条丝路，共同使命，相互融通。2015年，卢森堡货航将公司45周年庆典移至郑州举办。为此，公司专门定制了全新的波音747-8F全货机。当身披由波音公司完成的有史以来最大彩绘图的飞机飞抵郑州时，也标志着河南"空中丝绸之路"米兰—郑州航线加密至每周2班，卢森堡货航在郑州新郑国际机场的运力达到每周13班，海外航点数达到7个（卢森堡、米兰、芝加哥、小松、巴库、新加坡、吉隆坡），覆盖亚太、横跨欧美的航线网络布局已初步形成。

表：2015年河南"空中丝绸之路"航班网络

航班	周次
卢森堡—郑州	5班
卢森堡—巴库—郑州—芝加哥	1班
卢森堡—郑州—小松—芝加哥	1班
新加坡—吉隆坡—郑州—芝加哥	2班
芝加哥—郑州—新加坡—吉隆坡—卢森堡	2班
米兰—郑州	2班

资料来源：河南航投

日趋增多的航点、日渐丰富的航线网络展示着河南"空中丝绸之路"正变得更加顺通发达。2015年11月23日，随着卢森堡货航全货机第438次在郑州新郑国际机场停落，全年5万吨运输目标提前超额实现。卢森堡货航在累计国际货运量、国际货运航线数、航班数量、国际通航点等多项指标上的排名均跃居郑州新郑国际机场首位，为郑州航空港实验区打造成为国际航空货运枢纽做出了新贡献，郑州—卢森堡"双枢纽"成为河南依靠蓝天对外开放的重要战略支撑点。

its 45th birthday in Zhengzhou, Cargolux Airlines International specially customized the new Boeing 747-8F all cargo carrier. The Boeing air flight's arrival in Zhengzhou also marked the incorporation of the Milan-Zhengzhou route into the "Silk Road in the Air". The Milan-Zhengzhou route has 2 flights per week, and the capacity of Cargolux Airlines International in Zhengzhou Xinzheng International Airport has reached 13 flights per week, including 7 overseas flight points (Luxembourg, Milan, Chicago, Komatsu, Baku, Singapore, and Kuala Lumpur). The flight network covering the Asia-Pacific region, Europe and America has already formed.

Table: "Silk Road in the Air" Flight Network in Henan in 2015

Flight Route	Flight(s) /Week
Luxembourg- Zhengzhou	5
Luxembourg - Baku - Zhengzhou - Chicago	1
Luxembourg - Zhengzhou - Komatsu - Chicago	1
Singapore - Kuala Lumpur - Zhengzhou - Chicago	2
Chicago- Zhengzhou- Singapore-Kuala Lumpur-Luxembourg	2
Milan - Zhengzhou	2

Source: Henan Civil Aviation Development and Investment Co., Ltd.

The increasing number of navigation points and the increasingly rich route network show that Henan's "Silk Road in the Air" is steadily developing. On November 23, 2015, with the landing of the entire fleet of 438 cargo planes of Cargolux Airlines International at Zhengzhou Xinzheng International Airport, the annual transportation target of 50,000 tons was exceeded ahead of schedule. On the list of flights to Zhengzhou Xinzheng International Airport, Cargolux Airlines International ranked first in accumulative international freight, international cargo airlines, number of flights, and international navigation points making the Zhengzhou Airport Economy Zone an international air cargo hub. The Zhengzhou-Luxembourg "double hubs" became the strategic point for Henan's opening up to the outside world via the blue sky.

三、河南"空中丝绸之路"的谋划发展

河南"空中丝绸之路"的开通既是河南省注重航空产业发展的成果，同时也为全省航空业及航空经济等新经济业态的发展提供了动力。河南"空中丝绸之路"的建设从物流合作向枢纽建设、航线拓展、产业培育、金融创新、经贸交流、人文往来等领域进行全方位突破，与全省经济社会高质量发展形成了积极互动。

2016年，河南省为进一步激发航空业在全省经济社会发展中的引领作用，加强了对航空产业发展的规划。同年1月，河南省政府下发了《关于进一步加快民航业发展的意见》（简称《意见》），明确提出要"坚持东联西进、贯通全球、构建枢纽的战略导向，以郑州航空枢纽为支点构建'空中丝绸之路'"的指导思想，以此来推动本省航空经济的发展，促进经济结构调整、产业升级和城镇化建设。

> 专栏：《关于进一步加快民航业发展的意见》为河南"空中丝绸之路"制定的规划任务与目标
>
> 《意见》提出，要以郑州航空枢纽为战略支点，拓展优化航线网络。
>
> 突出郑州机场国际航空货运枢纽、国内大型航空枢纽的战略定位，按照"货运为先、国际为先、以干为先"的总体思路，加快构建东联西进、贯通全球的航线网络。
>
> 积极融入、主动服务国家"一带一路"倡议，按照"开美、稳欧、拓非、联亚"的主攻方向，着力开发连接全球主要货运机场和发达经济体的国际航线；推进实施"郑州—卢森堡"双枢纽战略，拓展豫欧空中通道；加大力度开辟郑州至"一带一路"沿线国家（地区）的客运、货运航线。

III. The Plan of the "Silk Road in the Air" in Henan Province

The founding of Henan's "Silk Road in the Air" was the outcome of Henan's emphasis on the development of aviation industry and it provides a driving force for the development of the aviation industry, aviation economy and other economic initiatives in Henan Province. The construction of the "Silk Road in the Air" has achieved breakthroughs in logistics cooperation, hub construction, route expansion, industrial cultivation, financial innovation, economic and cultural exchanges, and other fields. The "Silk Road in the Air" has facilitated high-quality development of the economy and society of the province.

In 2016, Henan Province updated its plans for the development of the aviation industry in order to further emphasize the aviation in Henan's economic and social development. In January, the Henan Provincial Government issued *Opinions on Further Accelerating the Development of Civil Aviation Industry*, which emphasized the strategy of connecting the East and the West, linking the whole world, building the hub and making Zhengzhou a key aviation point. The opinions were aimed at boosting the development of Henan's aviation economy, promoting the adjustment of the Province's economic structure, and upgrading industrial and urban construction projects.

> **Column: *Opinions on Further Accelerating the Development of the Civil Aviation Industry* Formulates Planning Tasks and Objectives for Henan's "Silk Road in the Air"**
>
> *Opinions on Further Accelerating the Development of the Civil Aviation Industry* proposed to use Zhengzhou's aviation hub as a strategic fulcrum to expand and optimize the route network.
>
> The strategic positioning of Zhengzhou Airport as an international air cargo hub and a large domestic aviation hub should be highlighted. According to the general idea of "cargo first, internationality first, and action first", Henan should speed up the construction of a route network

> 充分发挥国际客运航线以客为主、客货兼营的优势，积极培育国际客运航线。持续扩大国内客运航线网络，推广郑州—上海"空中快线"模式，加密、优化郑州至国内主要枢纽机场的航班。
>
> 优化网络结构，加强国际和国内、干线和支线、货运和客运航线间的衔接，构建货运航线与客运航线、航空运输网络与陆路交通紧密衔接、协调发展的枢纽网络格局。
>
> 培育国际航空货运枢纽竞争力，推进国际航空物流中心建设。着力培育提升郑州机场全货运航线的竞争优势，力争2020年全货机通航城市达到50个以上。

围绕河南"空中丝绸之路"建设目标，河南在坚持发展航空运输和航空物流等主业的基础上，着手完善航空产业链布局。

推动航空租赁业发展。2016年1月，河南航投与立陶宛AviaAM租赁集团为开展融资租赁项目合作进行会谈，签署了战略合作协议。5月24日，双方在郑州正式签署合资合同，其中中方占股49%，外方占股51%，合资公司将主要在飞机、航材设备及基础设施建设等领域开展业务。12月8日，阿维亚融资租赁（中国）有限公司（AviaAM Financial Leasing China Co., Ltd.）揭牌暨项目签约仪式在郑州举行，当日即获得16架飞机租赁的国际业务。这标志着河南航空及金融产业向产融结合、创新发展迈出了历史性的一步，填补了河南金融资本市场的一项空白。

设立航空产业基金。2016年4月，河南民航产业基金管理有限公司正式成立，作为河南唯一一家致力于民航产业发展的基金公司，积极引导社会资本参与投资民航业，成立了两只管理规模共为22亿元的基金，募资到位1000万元。

当年，河南"空中丝绸之路"的主业继续绽放光彩。2016年，河南

connecting the East and the West with the whole world.

Henan actively integrates and serves the nation's Belt and Road Initiative. In accordance with the main direction of "paving the way to the American market, stabilizing the European market, expanding the African market and connecting the Asian market", Henan focuses on developing international air routes that connect major cargo airports and developed economies around the world. It promotes the implementation of the "Zhengzhou-Luxembourg" double-hubs strategy and the expansion of the air routes between Europe and Henan. More efforts should be made to open up passenger and freight routes from Zhengzhou to the countries and regions along the Belt and Road route.

Henan actively cultivates international passenger routes, and will continue to expand its domestic passenger airline network, promote the Zhengzhou-Shanghai "air express" model and optimize flights from Zhengzhou to major domestic hub airports.

Henan will improve its network structure, strengthen connectivity between international and domestic airports, trunk and branch lines, and between freight and passenger routes. Its aim is to build a hub network where freight and passenger routes, along with air and land transport networks are closely connected, and develop in a coordinated manner.

Henan will foster the competitiveness of international air cargo hubs and build international aviation logistics centers. Efforts should be made to cultivate and improve the competitive advantages of Zhengzhou Airport in all-cargo routes, aiming at reaching more than 50 navigation cities by 2020.

Centering on the goal of building the "Silk Road in the Air", Henan has persisted in developing air transport and aviation logistics, as well as improving the layout of the aviation industry chain.

The development of the aviation leasing industry should also be promoted. In January 2016, Henan Civil Aviation Development and Investment Co., Ltd. and Lithuania AviaAM Leasing Group held talks on the cooperation of financial leasing projects and signed a strategic cooperation agreement. On May 24, the

"空中丝绸之路"全年累计执飞航班超过650班，货运吞吐量突破10.7万吨，与上年同比增加4.2万吨。累计货运量、国际货运航线数、航班数量、国际通航点等四项指标在郑州新郑国际机场继续保持首位。

进入2017年，河南"空中丝绸之路"在空间与内容上继续实施创新。河南省政府和企业先后与泰国正大集团、微笑航空、皇雀航空等知名企业先后签署合作协议，在运输、物流、贸易、金融、旅游等领域达成多项共识。河南"空中丝绸之路"推动河南与泰国之间的合作进入了一个新的阶段。

与此同时，河南"空中丝绸之路"在全球航空货运市场中保持高速增长。仅在2017年第一季度，郑州—卢森堡航线累计执飞航班148班，同期增加30班，货运吞吐量约2.44万吨，同期增加47%。郑州—卢森堡、郑州—米兰、卢森堡—郑州—芝加哥3条航线市场辐射范围覆盖欧、亚、北美三大洲的23个国家100多个城市，集疏的货物达10余类200多个品种。

2017年是中国与卢森堡正式建立外交关系45周年。河南"空中丝绸之路"乘势而上。6月12日，卢森堡货航和河南航投在北京正式签署了合资合同，合资成立以郑州为基地的本土货运航空公司，并以此来集聚更多的客、货运航空，航材维修制造，物流货代，地面服务，金融资本，电子商务等优势资源，进一步做大做强河南"空中丝绸之路"的"双枢纽"。6月13日，河南省与卢森堡签署了《关于在河南开展签证便利业务谅解备忘录》，卢森堡驻华大使馆将在郑州开展飞行签证业务，向河南省及周边省份居民直接提供赴欧盟签证的便利化服务。河南"空中丝绸之路"上再添经贸文化往来新举措。

"时间的刻度因其记载的重大事件而具有特殊意义。" 2017年6月14日是河南"空中丝绸之路"建设中一个值得铭记的日子。中国国家主席习近平在会见卢森堡首相贝泰尔时强调，中方支持建设郑州—卢森堡"空中丝绸之路"，要加强文化、教育、体育等人文交流，提高人员往

two sides formally signed a joint venture contract in Zhengzhou, in which the Chinese side holds 49% of the shares and the foreign side holds 51%. The joint venture company will mainly conduct business in the fields of aircraft, aviation equipment and infrastructure construction. On December 8, AviaAM Financial Leasing China Co., Ltd. was inaugurated and the signing ceremony of the project was held in Zhengzhou. On the same day, AviaAM Financial Leasing China Co., Ltd. obtained the international business of leasing 16 aircraft. This historic step marks the integration of Henan's aviation and financial industries, and fills a gap in Henan's financial capital market.

In April 2016, Henan Civil Aviation Industry Fund Management Co., Ltd. was formally established. As the only fund company dedicated to the development of the civil aviation industry in Henan Province, Henan Civil Aviation Industry Fund Management Co., Ltd. actively guides social capital to participate in investment in the civil aviation industry. Two funds with a total management size of 2.2 billion yuan were set up, and 10 million yuan has been raised.

Since that time, Henan's "Silk Road in the Air" initiatives have continued to flourish. In 2016, the "Silk Road in the Air" in Henan facilitated more than 650 flights and a cargo throughput of 107,000 tons, an increase of 42,000 tons over the previous year. The total international freight volume, the number of international freight routes, the number of flights and the international navigation destinations continue to maintain the first place in Zhengzhou Xinzheng International Airport.

In 2017, Henan's "Silk Road in the Air" continued to make innovations in logistics and trade. The Henan Provincial Government and domestic enterprises have signed cooperation agreements with Thailand Charoen Pokphand Group, Thai Smile, Nok Air and numerous other enterprises, and reached a number of consensuses in the fields of transportation, logistics, trade, finance and tourism. The "Silk Road in the Air" has pushed the cooperation between Henan and Thailand into a new stage.

Meanwhile, Henan's "Silk Road in the Air" has maintained rapid growth in the global air cargo market. In the first quarter of 2017 alone, the Zhengzhou-Luxembourg route operated a total of 148 flights, an increase of 30 flights over the previous period, and a cargo throughput of about 24,400 tons, an increase of

来便利化水平。这是中国国家领导人首次在公开场合提出和使用"空中丝绸之路"的概念,向世界传达出这样的信息:中国通过郑州与卢森堡的合作,建设与全世界扩大贸易和全方位合作的"空中丝绸之路",是对"一带一路"倡议内涵的丰富和拓展。

在如此难得的历史机遇面前,河南进一步明确要将郑州—卢森堡"空中丝绸之路"打造成为引领中部、服务全国、联通欧亚、辐射世界的空中经济廊道,推动河南实现更高水平的对外开放,在支撑"一带一路"建设和服务全国大局中发挥更大作用。为此,河南制定实施了《郑州—卢森堡"空中丝绸之路"建设专项规划(2017—2025年)》和《推进郑州—卢森堡"空中丝绸之路"建设工作方案》,提出要夯实基础,提升枢纽功能,拓展布局构建航线网络,强化合作培育特色产业,扩大开放推动经济贸易。

> **专栏:河南"空中丝绸之路"建设新蓝图**
>
> 《郑州—卢森堡"空中丝绸之路"建设专项规划(2017—2025年)》明确提出了提升"双枢纽"功能、构建国际航线网络、培育航空特色产业、推动经贸交流合作、强化金融服务保障、深化人文交流合作6项主要任务,争取到2025年,郑州—卢森堡"空中丝绸之路"与郑州航空港经济综合实验区同步全面建成,郑州基本建成国家中心城市和国际枢纽城市,郑州、卢森堡成为亚太和欧美物流集散分拨基地,在支撑国家"一带一路"建设中发挥核心作用。卢森堡货航及合资货航公司航空货运量超过100万吨,航空维修、航空租赁、金融服务、跨境贸易等关联产业形成集聚发展态势,郑州—卢森堡"空中丝绸之路"成为引领中部、服务全国、连通欧亚、辐射全球的空中经济廊道。
>
> 《推进郑州—卢森堡"空中丝绸之路"建设工作方案》侧重

47%. The market radiation of the Zhengzhou-Luxembourg, Zhengzhou-Milan, and Luxembourg-Zhengzhou-Chicago routes covers 23 countries and more than 100 cities in Europe, Asia, and North America, incorporating 10 categories and more than 200 varieties of cargo.

The year 2017 marks the 45th anniversary of the official establishment of diplomatic relations between China and Luxembourg. Henan's "Silk Road in the Air" is building on the momentum. On June 12, Cargolux Airlines International and Henan Civil Aviation Development and Investment Co., Ltd. formally signed the joint venture contract in Beijing, which covers the Zhengzhou-based development of passenger and cargo aviation, aviation material maintenance and manufacturing, logistics freight forwarders, ground maintenance services, financial capital, and E-commerce resource advantages, and further develops and expands Henan's "Silk Road in the Air" and "double hubs". On June 13, Henan Province and Luxembourg signed the *Memorandum of Understanding on Visa Facilitation Services in Henan Province*. The embassy of Luxembourg in China will carry out flight visa business in Zhengzhou, providing convenient services for residents of Henan Province and its neighboring provinces to obtain visas to the European Union. Henan's "Silk Road in the Air" has added new measures for economic and cultural exchanges.

"The scale of time has special significance because of the important events it records." The date of June 14, 2017 is a memorable day in the construction of the "Silk Road in the Air" in Henan Province. When meeting with Luxembourg Prime Minister Xavier Bettel, Chinese President Xi Jinping stressed that China supports the building of the Zhengzhou-Luxembourg "Silk Road in the Air" and that cultural, educational and sports exchanges should be strengthened. This is the first time that Chinese leaders publicly put forward the concept of "Silk Road in the Air", conveying that China is establishing all-round cooperation with the world, beginning with the cooperation between Zhengzhou and Luxembourg. Henan's "Silk Road in the Air" enriches and develops the connotation of the Belt and Road Initiative.

Facing such a rare opportunity, Henan decided to make the Zhengzhou-Luxembourg "Silk Road in the Air" a model of leading central China's economy, delivering services across the country, linking Europe with Asia, navigating the

> 明确短、中期落实实施的13项重点工作安排，明确建设时间表、路线图和责任人。重点内容包括开通郑州至卢森堡直飞洲际客运航线，批准运营卢森堡货航合资货运航空公司，投入使用卢森堡飞行签证中心，设立药品进口口岸，深入对接双方物流信息，全面开展金融合作和文化旅游交流等。

作为落实河南"空中丝绸之路"建设专项规划和工作方案的具体举措，河南航投、中航信托股份有限公司、河南省现代服务业产业投资基金共同成立了中原丝路基金。2017年8月23日，中原丝路基金在河南郑州正式成立。该基金聚焦国家"一带一路"建设框架下的"设施联通""贸易畅通""资金融通""民心相通"四大领域，多元化投资包括机场建设、临空产业园、物流园区等在内的基础设施，以及民航相关产业、省内贸易产业链、贸易金融服务、文化旅游、生态旅游等具有良好发展前景的企业和项目。

此时，河南"空中丝绸之路"具备了"天时"与"地利"，这些优势的汇集也成就了"人和"。2017年9月13日，由卢森堡21家重量级企业组成的大型经贸团到访河南郑州，参加河南—卢森堡"一带一路"经济合作论坛。与会者认为河南"空中丝绸之路"是河南省对外开放的重要平台，也是双方合作的希望和机遇。期间，河南贸促会与卢森堡大公国商会签署合作谅解备忘录，河南航投与卢森堡商会签署了合作备忘录。中—卢两国的企业家借助此次论坛共同探讨了未来互利共赢新机遇，期待河南"空中丝绸之路"能够推动河南与卢森堡的经贸联系再上一个新台阶。

同一时期，河南"空中丝绸之路"建设继续在完善航空产业链内容上下功夫。2017年8月，立陶宛BAA航空培训学院成为河南设立飞行员培训中心的战略合作伙伴。BAA航空培训学院是欧洲地区具有较大影响力的飞行领域培训中心，通过在培训技术和管理等领域与河南展开全面

world economic corridor and supporting China in the construction of the Belt and Road Initiative. For this purpose, Henan drafted *The Zhengzhou-Luxembourg "Silk Road in the Air" Construction Special Planning (2017—2025)* and *The Work Plan for Promoting the Construction of the Zhengzhou-Luxembourg "Silk Road in the Air"*. Henan put forward a solid foundation for expanding its hub function and network layout, strengthening cooperation, cultivating domestic industry, and promoting trade.

> **Column: Blueprint of Henan's "Silk Road in the Air" Construction**
>
> *The Zhengzhou-Luxembourg "Silk Road in the Air" Construction Special Planning (2017—2025)* clearly puts forward six major tasks: enhancing the function of "double hubs", building an international airline network, cultivating the characteristic aviation industry, promoting economic and trade exchanges and cooperation, strengthening financial service guarantees, and deepening cultural and educational exchanges and cooperation. Henan has labored to complete the Zhengzhou-Luxembourg "Silk Road in the Air" and Zhengzhou Airport Economy Zone, making Zhengzhou an international hub city. Zhengzhou and Luxembourg have become logistics distribution bases in the Asia-Pacific region, Europe and America, and will support China in the construction of the "Belt and Road" Initiative in 2025. The air cargo volume of Cargolux Airlines International and joint venture cargo transport company exceeded 1 million tons, and related industries such as aviation maintenance, aviation leasing, financial services and cross-border trade formed a trend of agglomeration and development. The "Silk Road in the Air" between Zhengzhou and Luxembourg has become an economic corridor, leading the central China, serving the whole country, connecting Europe and Asia, and extending to the whole world.
>
> *The Work Plan for Promoting the Construction of the Zhengzhou-Luxembourg "Silk Road in the Air"* focuses on defining 13 key work arrangements for implementation in the short and medium term, as well as the construction schedule, road map and responsible persons. The key contents include: opening a direct intercontinental passenger route from

合作，将为中国民用航空储备专业飞行人员。

2017年一系列精彩纷呈的合作与开拓让河南"空中丝绸之路"取得了令人瞩目的成绩。卢森堡货航在郑州的三条洲际货运航线的航班密度由每周定期13班加密至16班，旺季加开包机航班增加至每周23班，新增了亚特兰大、伦敦、阿拉木图、土库曼巴希、第比利斯、萨拉戈萨6个通航点，通航点总数达到14个，累计执飞航班789班，货运量14.7万吨，超额完成全年12万吨的目标。

2018年，河南"空中丝绸之路"再添新里程碑。4月16日，卢森堡旅游签证（郑州）便捷服务平台正式揭牌运行。郑州成为除北京、上海之外，中国境内第三个能够办理卢森堡签证的城市，实现了河南省办理签证业务零的突破，丰富了河南"空中丝绸之路"的内涵。7月，《关于开通郑州至卢森堡国际客运航线的合作意向书》在卢森堡首相府签署，这进一步推进了两国人文交流，为民心相通蓄势增能。河南航投与俄罗斯乌克图斯航空公司签署合作谅解备忘录，商讨开展股权合作，开通郑州—莫斯科航线，设立航空科学研究院、航空人才培训中心以及建立中俄合资航空燃油公司等事宜。10月，《河南航投与比利时航空公司战略合作框架协议》在比利时签署。根据协议，河南与比利时将强化航空领域合作，推动飞机租赁、航空金融等相关配套业务开展，整合比利时和河南文化旅游市场资源，促进两地高端服务业升级。11月，主题为"联结世界与金融丝绸之路"卢森堡金融推介会在郑州举行，卢森堡证券交易所等40余家金融服务机构代表汇聚郑州，与河南省投资类企业和"走出去"工商企业代表，共商合作机会。这是卢森堡首次在北京、上海之外的中国内地城市召开此类盛会，表明河南"空中丝绸之路"在资金融通方面迈出了重要一步，推动了河南省深化金融服务业开放和郑州国家中心城市建设的步伐。

2019年，河南"空中丝绸之路"继续精心绘制工笔画。4月3日，卢森堡—郑州—布达佩斯国际货运航线开通，卢森堡货航在郑州新郑国

> Zhengzhou to Luxembourg, approving the operation of a joint cargo airline from Luxembourg, putting into use the Luxembourg flight visa center, setting up a drug import port, make in-depth efforts to build well-aligned channels for logistics information sharing of the two sides, and carrying out financial cooperation and cultural and tourism exchanges in an all-round way.

On August 23, 2017, Henan Civil Aviation Development and Investment Co., Ltd., Avic Trust Co., Ltd. and Henan Modern Service Industry Investment Fund jointly established the Zhongyuan Silk Road Fund, in order to implement the special plan and work program of Henan's "Silk Road in the Air" construction. The Fund focuses on construction under the framework of "facilities connection", "smooth trade", "financial support" and "interpersonal communication". It also focuses on the infrastructure construction, including airport, airport industrial parks, and logistics parks, as well as the civil aviation industry, the trade industry chain, financial services, cultural tourism and eco-tourism projects and enterprises.

On September 13, 2017, a large economic and trade delegation from 21 major enterprises of Luxembourg visited Zhengzhou, and participated in Henan-Luxembourg "Belt and Road" Economic Cooperation Forum. The participants agreed that the "Silk Road in the Air" in Henan was an important platform for the opening up of Henan Province, as well as an opportunity for cooperation between the two sides. During this visit, both the Airlines Council for the Promotion of International Trade and Henan Civil Aviation Development and Investment Co., Ltd. signed a *Memorandum of Understanding on Cooperation* with the Chamber of Commerce of the Grand Duchy of Luxembourg. Entrepreneurs from China and Luxembourg took advantage of the forum to jointly explore new opportunities for mutual benefit, hoping that the "Silk Road in the Air" in Henan could push the economic and trade ties between Henan and Luxembourg to a new level.

At the same time, Henan continued to make improvements to the "Silk Road in the Air" aviation industry chain. In August 2017, Lithuania BAA Aviation Training Institute became the strategic partner of Henan setting up pilot training

际机场的通航点增至15个，河南"空中丝绸之路"在中、东欧打开了一个新窗口。6月25日，南航河南公司开通了郑州—伦敦洲际定期客运往返航线，这是郑州首条直达西欧的定期客运航线。7月1日，卢森堡—郑州—厦门—洛杉矶货运航线正式开通，这是河南"空中丝绸之路"开辟的又一条第五航权航线，洛杉矶成为继芝加哥、亚特兰大之后，卢森堡货航在北美市场的又一重要通航点。以郑州为中心，"一点连三洲，一线串欧美"的航空货运网络进一步加密。

center. BAA Aviation Training Institute is an influential flight training center in Europe. Through comprehensive cooperation with Henan Province in the fields of training technology and management, BAA will reserve professional flight personnel for China's civil aviation.

In 2017, a series of cooperative ventures made remarkable achievements in Henan's "Silk Road in the Air". Three of Cargolux's intercontinental cargo airlines in Zhengzhou increased their regular flights from 13 to 16 per week, increased the number of charter flights to 23 per week during the busy seasons, and opened new routes to Atlanta, London, Alma-Ata, Turkmenbashi, Tbilisi, and Zaragoza, with a total of 14 navigation points and 789 flights delivering 147,000 tons of freight volume, surpassing its annual target of 120,000 tons.

In 2018, a new milestone was added to Henan's "Silk Road in the Air". On April 16, Luxembourg Tourist Visa (Zhengzhou) Convenient Service Platform was officially launched. In addition to Beijing and Shanghai, Zhengzhou has become the third city in China to institute a tourist visa program with Luxembourg. In July, *The Letter of Intent on Opening International Passenger Routes between Zhengzhou and Luxembourg* was signed in the Prime Minister's office of Luxembourg, which further promoted intercultural exchanges. Henan Civil Aviation Development and Investment Co., Ltd. signed a memorandum of understanding in cooperation with Russia's Uktus Airlines, discussing matters such as equity cooperation, the opening of a Zhengzhou-Moscow route, the establishment of an aviation research institute, aviation talent training center and a Sino-Russian joint venture aviation fuel company. In October, *The Strategic Cooperation Framework Agreement between Henan Airlines and Belgian Airlines* was signed in Belgium. According to the agreement, Henan and Belgium will strengthen cooperation in the field of aviation, promote the development of relevant supporting businesses such as aircraft leasing and aviation finance, integrate the cultural tourism market resources of Belgium and Henan, and promote the upgrading of high-end service industries in the two countries. In November, the Luxembourg Financial Promotion Conference, with the theme of "Silk Road Connecting the World and Finance", was held in Zhengzhou. Representatives of more than 40 financial service institutions, including the Luxembourg Stock Exchange, gathered in Zhengzhou to discuss cooperation

河南"空中丝绸之路"的阶段性成果超出合作双方的预期，也肩负起实现未来更为重要发展目标的历史使命。2019年4月8日，在第十三届中国（河南）国际投资贸易洽谈会期间，河南"空中丝绸之路"未来将深化产业、经贸和人文交流合作，成为2019"空中丝绸之路"经济合作论坛的共识。6月，河南省发布了《关于以"一带一路"建设为统领加快构建内陆开放高地的意见》，明确提出要通过深化郑州和卢森堡"双枢纽"战略合作，优化通航点布局，加密国际货运航线航班等举措，提升河南开放通道优势。

opportunities with representatives of investment enterprises, and "Going Abroad" industrial and commercial enterprises in Henan Province. This was the first time for Luxembourg to hold such a grand gathering in a city outside Beijing or Shanghai in Chinese mainland. It shows that the "Silk Road in the Air" in Henan Province has taken an important step in developing the financial service industry in Henan Province and promoting Zhengzhou as an international center.

In 2019, a more elaborate stroke was added to the picture of the "Silk Road in the Air" in Henan. On April 3, the Luxembourg-Zhengzhou-Budapest international cargo route was opened, the destinations of Cargolux Airlines International from Zhengzhou Xinzheng International Airport increased to 15, and Henan's "Silk Road in the Air" opened a new window in central and eastern Europe. On June 25, China Southern Airlines Co., Ltd. opened an intercontinental regular passenger service between Zhengzhou and London, the first regular passenger service between Zhengzhou and Western Europe. On July 1, the Luxembourg-Zhengzhou-Xiamen-Los Angeles freight route was officially opened, becoming another "Silk Road in the Air" trade route observing the Fifth Freedom, and adding an important navigation point in North America. The air cargo network "connecting three continents at one point" was further strengthened.

The initial achievements of the "Silk Road in the Air" in Henan have exceeded the expectations of both sides and have inspired the mission of realizing future strategic goals. On April 8, 2019, during the 13th China (Henan) International Investment and Trade Fair, Henan's "Silk Road in the Air" paved the way for future industrial, economic, trade and cultural exchanges. In June, Henan Province released *The Opinions on Accelerating the Construction of Inland Opening up with the Direction of Belt and Road Construction*, which clearly proposed that the advantages of Henan as an open channel be enhanced by deepening the strategic cooperation of "double hubs" between Zhengzhou and Luxembourg, optimizing the layout of navigable points, and setting up international freight routes and flights.

In order to better realize its goals and missions, the "Silk Road in the Air" in Henan needs new impetus and measures. On June 14, 2019, Longhao Airlines the first cargo airline based in Henan, officially launched its regular cargo route

如何更好地实现目标与使命,河南"空中丝绸之路"需要有新的动力和举措。2019年6月14日,河南首家本土基地货运航空公司中原龙浩航空公司正式执飞郑州—广州定期货运航线,掀开了河南"空中丝绸之路"建设的崭新一页。它标志着河南"空中丝绸之路"实现了国际航线"大动脉"与国内中短程航线"毛细血管"的连通。通过打造中国内陆、环太平洋货运航线网络、中国与东南亚的空中物流走廊等新航线网络,河南"空中丝绸之路"的通达性和便利性得到有力的提升。随即,中原龙浩航空有限公司开通了广州—武汉、西安—淮安两条货运航线;10月,中原龙浩航空有限公司开通了郑州—合肥—河内—郑州定期货运航线;11月,开通了武汉—深圳航线;12月,开通了郑州—济南—大阪—郑州、武汉—大阪两条国际货运航线。河南"空中丝绸之路"的航线运输网络更加丰富,运输活力更为强劲。

专栏:河南中原龙浩航空公司的发展现状与前景规划

自2019年5月收购重组中原龙浩后,河南航投通过组建高质量管理运营队伍确保航空公司运行安全平稳有序。先后选聘具有民航监管机构任职经历及大型航空公司丰富高管经验的人才,担任公司董事长兼总经理;招聘各岗位员工77人,其中核心工作人员47人、成熟机长及副驾驶7人。

目前,中原龙浩航空公司共有B737CL机型飞机6架,在郑州投放过夜飞机2架,串飞运力3架,飞机日利用率达到5.47小时(2020年8月,飞机利用率超过6.24小时,创运行以来最佳水平);实现营业收入19244.05万元,生产运营稳中向好。

为应对新冠肺炎疫情期间国际航空货运市场发展需求,中原龙浩航空公司谋划以"包机—湿租—购买"的形式引进2架南航波音747货机及其配套保障能力,2020年10月在郑州首航,以加快国

from Zhengzhou to Guangzhou, turning a new page in the construction of Henan's "Silk Road in the Air". The "Silk Road in the Air" connects the "arteries" of international routes and the "capillaries" of domestic short and medium routes. The connectivity and convenience of Henan's "Silk Road in the Air" have been enhanced by building new air route networks such as in China's inland network and the Pacific Rim freight route network, as well as the air logistics corridor between China and Southeast Asia. Subsequently, Longhao Airlines opened two freight routes: from Guangzhou to Wuhan, and from Xi'an to Huai'an. In October, Longhao Airlines opened the Zhengzhou-Hefei-Hanoi-Zhengzhou scheduled freight route, in November, the Wuhan-Shenzhen freight route, and in December, two international freight routes: Zhengzhou-Jinan-Osaka-Zhengzhou and Wuhan-Osaka. The "Silk Road in the Air" in Henan is diversifying its air transport network and strengthening its transport vitality.

Column: The Development and Vision of Longhao Airlines Co., Ltd.

Since the acquisition and restructuring of Longhao Airlines Co., Ltd. in May 2019, Henan Civil Aviation Development and Investment Co., Ltd has established a high-quality management and operation team to ensure the smooth and orderly operation of the airline company. The company has successively selected and recruited personnel with experience in civil aviation regulatory bodies or in large airlines to serve as chairman and general manager of the company; and has recruited 77 employees, including 47 core staff members, and 7mature captains and co-pilots.

At present, Longhao Airlines Co., Ltd. has 6 B737CL airplanes, 2 overnight airplanes in Zhengzhou, and 3 airplanes in tandem capacity. The daily utilization rate of the airplanes reached 5.47 hours (in August 2020, the utilization rate of the airplanes exceeded 6.24 hours, which is the highest level since operation), and the operating income reached 192.44 million yuan, with stable and positive production and operation.

In order to meet the development demand of international air cargo market during the epidemic period of COVID-19, Longhao Airlines Co., Ltd. planed to introduce two Boeing 747 cargo planes and the supporting

际和洲际航空货运市场开发速度。

为全力支持郑州国际航空货运枢纽建设，中原龙浩航空公司聘请了国际航空知名咨询机构——盖安德战略咨询公司及行业专家制定了未来5年发展规划，即：

在机队组建方面，预计到2023年公司机队规模将达到23架，到2025年公司机队规模达到29架，主要机型包括B737-800货机、B767货机、B747/B777洲际宽体货机。

在网络规划方面，预计2021年以填补郑州国际货运航线网络的空白区域为重点，开通郑州始发至南亚、中亚、中东等地区的货运航线。2022年以全球布局为重点，推动构建"以郑州为中心，大、中、小机型高低搭配，航线规划长短相宜"的航空货运网络，以小机型深挖国内货运航线运营潜力，建成覆盖东亚、东南亚的货运航线网络；以中机型开通至中亚、南亚、中东等地的货运航线；以大机型开通至欧美、非洲等地区的货运航线，形成覆盖世界主要发达经济体和新兴市场的网络辐射能力。

在人力规划方面，公司将新增引进各类员工800人（其中包括成熟飞行员160人、机务人员300人、签派人员60人等），预计到2022年末公司人员规模达到1100人，到2025年末公司人员规模将达到1550人。

capacity in the form of "charter freighter–wet lease–purchase". It is expected to be launched in Zhengzhou before October 2020 to accelerate the development of the international and intercontinental air cargo market.

In order to fully support the construction of Zhengzhou international air cargo hub, Longhao Airlines Co., Ltd. has engaged GandW CONSULTING, the well-known international aviation consulting organization and other experts to formulate the development plan for the next five years. The following are the details of the plan.

Fleet size is expected to reach 23 in 2023, and 29 in 2025, including the B737-800 cargo aircraft, B767 cargo aircraft, and B747/B777 intercontinental widebody cargo aircraft.

In terms of network planning, Longhao Airlines Co., Ltd. will focus on filling the gaps in Zhengzhou's international freight network and open freight routes from Zhengzhou to South Asia, Central Asia, the Middle East and other regions in 2021. In 2022, focusing on global distribution, Longhao Airlines Co., Ltd. will push for the establishment of an air cargo network with Zhengzhou as the center, and the large, medium and small airplanes matching the route length", so as to tap the operational potential of domestic freight routes with small aircraft, to build a network of cargo routes covering East and Southeast Asia; to open cargo routes to Central Asia, South Asia and the Middle East with medium-sized aircraft; and to open cargo routes to Europe, America and Africa with large-sized aircraft. It focuses on the formation of the network with radiation capacity covering the world's major developed economies and emerging markets.

In terms of human resource, the company will recruit 800 new employees (including 160 mature pilots, 300 crew members and 60 dispatch personnel). Longhao Airlines Co., Ltd. is expected to have 1,100 personnel by the end of 2022, and 1,550 employees by the end of 2025.

第二章

联通跨五洲：河南"空中丝绸之路"的成效

Chapter 2

Connecting Five Continents: the Achievements of the "Silk Road in the Air" in Henan Province

河南"空中丝绸之路"随着中国"一带一路"建设的发展而不断地延展,已经成为河南省融入中国"一带一路"建设的龙头和对外开放的靓丽名片,在国际、国家与省级等多层面为推动社会经济发展发挥出积极的作用,被誉为"'一带一路'建设推动开放型世界经济体系建设的一个样板工程"。

一、河南"空中丝绸之路"主业示范效应突出,拉动了合作双方航空运输业务实现共赢发展

航空运输是河南"空中丝绸之路"的主业,6年来,中—卢合作双方在主业领域均取得了巨大成效。

2014—2019年河南"空中丝绸之路"货运规模

河南"空中丝绸之路"的开通提升了卢森堡货航业内的领先地位。2014—2019年,卢森堡货航在河南"空中丝绸之路"的航班量由2班/周加密至18班/周,通航点由3个城市增至16个城市;航线覆盖欧、美、亚三大洲24个国家100多个城市;每年货物运输规模由1.44万吨增至12.52万吨,6年间增长了近9倍;货运种类也由单一传统轻工业品发展到高精尖的精密仪器、活体动物等10余大类200多个品种。实现利润4亿美

Along with the development of China's Belt and Road construction, the "Silk Road in the Air" in Henan Province has been continuously extended. It has become a leading part of China's construction of Belt and Road in Henan Province and a beautiful calling card for opening to the outside world. It has played an active role in promoting economic and social development at the international, national and provincial levels, and has been hailed as "a model project of 'Belt and Road' construction to promote the construction of an open world economic system".

I. The Demonstration Effect of Henan's "Silk Road in the Air" in Promoting the Win-Win Development of the Air Transport Business

Air transport is the main industry of the "Silk Road in the Air" in Henan. In the past six years, Luxembourg and China have made great achievements in this field.

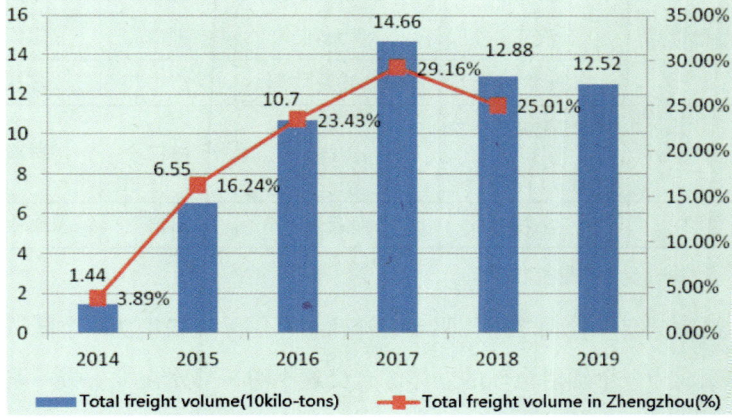

Volume of "Silk Road in the Air" Cargo in Henan from 2014 to 2019

Source: Statistics of Henan Civil Aviation Development and Investment Co., Ltd

The opening of the "Silk Road in the Air" in Henan Province has promoted Luxembourg's leading position in international cargo airlines. From 2014 to 2019, the number of flights of Cargolux Airlines International on the "Silk Road in

元，拉动公司在全球国际货运航空公司排名由合作初期的第九位提升到2018年的第六位。

表：卢森堡货航特殊货物运输

品类	货物	国家	进出口	次数
机械配件超大货物	发电站配件	意大利	进口	单次
	火车箱体配件	卢森堡	出口	多次
	机械配件	埃及	出口	单次
活体动物	种猪	荷兰	进口	多次
	矮种马	英国	进口	多次
	羊驼	/	进口	多次
	沙袋鼠	/	进口	/
新鲜产品	三文鱼	挪威	进口	多次
	龙虾	英国	进口	多次
	鲜切花	荷兰、厄瓜多尔	进口	多次
动力型货品	直升机	法国	进口	多次
	汽车	意大利	进口	多次
	飞机发动机	新加坡到欧洲	空空中转	多次
精密仪器	核磁共振医疗器械	美国	进口	单次
贵重物品	文物	卢森堡	出口	单次

资料来源：河南航投

河南"空中丝绸之路"驱动着郑州新郑国际机场正从一个区域性机场转变成为一个辐射全球的立体综合交通枢纽，郑州在"一带一路"沿线国家的航空枢纽中的地位日渐凸显。

郑州已经成为卢森堡货航在亚太地区最重要的基地和全球业务增长最快的站点，是该公司在亚洲的分拨中心和集散基地。

郑州新郑国际机场的客运、货运规模在中国中部地区排名持续保持双第一位置。2018年，在郑州机场运营的客运航空公司有44家，开通客

the Air" increased from 2 per week to 18 per week, and the number of navigable points increased from 3 to 16 cities. The airline covers more than 100 cities in 24 countries in Europe, America and Asia. The annual volume of goods transported increased from 14,400 tons to 125,200 tons, a nine-fold increase in six years. Freight categories have also developed from traditional light industrial products to sophisticated precision instruments, along with numerous other freight categories and hundreds of cargo types. With a profit of 400 million U.S. dollars, the company was promoted from the ninth place in the early stage of cooperation to the sixth place in 2018.

Table: Cargolux Airlines International special cargo transport

Category	Name of goods	Countries	Import and export	Number of times
Machinery accessories oversized cargo	Power station fittings	Italy	Import	Single time
	Train case fittings	Luxembourg	Export	Multi-times
	Machinery accessories	Egypt	Export	Single time
Live animals	Breeding pig	Netherlands	Import	Multi-times
	Pony	U. K.	Import	Multi-times
	Alpaca	/	Import	Multi-times
	Sand kangaroos	/	Import	/
Fresh produce	Salmon	Norway	Import	Multi-times
	Lobster	U. K.	Import	Multi-times
	Cut flowers	Netherlands, Ecuador	Import	Multi-times
Power goods	The helicopter	France	Import	Multi-times
	The car	Italy	Import	Multi-times
	Aircraft engine	Singapore to Europe	Air transfer	Multi-times
Precision instruments	Nuclear magnetic resonance (NMR)	The United States	Import	Single time
	Medical apparatus and instruments			
Precious products	Cultural relics	Luxembourg	Export	Single time

Source: Henan Civil Aviation Development and Investment Co., Ltd.

Henan's "Silk Road in the Air" is driving Zhengzhou Xinzheng International

运航线187条，航班架次有20万个，通航点有116个。在郑州机场运营的货运航空公司有21家，开通全货机航线34条，在全球前20位货运枢纽机场中，已开通16个航点。有151家货运代理企业在郑州机场开展业务，其中全球前10大货运代理企业已经有9家在郑州机场开展业务。郑州新郑国际机场在国际地区全货机航线数量、航班量、货运量排名仅次于北京、上海和广州三座城市。

表：郑州新郑国际机场客运、货运及航班起降架次

	2014	2015	2016	2017	2018	2019
旅客吞吐量（万人）	1580.5	1729.7	2076.3	2430	2733	2912.9
货运吞吐量（万吨）	37.04	40.33	45.67	50.27	51.5	52.2
总起降架次（万架次）	14.77	15.45	17.81	19.57	20.96	21.65

资料来源："中国的航空大都市：郑州航空港经济综合实验区"

郑州新郑国际机场服务标准成为引领行业发展的标杆。截至2020年4月，郑州新郑国际机场具备了七大口岸（即水果进口口岸、冰鲜水产品进口口岸、食用水生动物进口口岸、肉类进口口岸、活体动物进口口岸、国际邮件枢纽口岸、药品进口口岸）功能，是中国拥有口岸数量最多的内陆机场，也是中国最大的空运进口水果集散地和分拨中心。为提高国际货运进出口通关时效，郑州新郑国际机场设有保税区以及单一窗口电子报关清关系统，郑州"1210"海关监管模式成为中国跨境电商的模板，全省通关申报业务覆盖率达到90%以上，全面实施7×24小时客、货运通关保障。郑州新郑国际机场已经成为德国戴姆勒、宝马公司、高端汽车零配件，以及微软公司、联想集团生产的电子产品的重要集散地。据统计，2018年，德国戴姆勒、宝马汽车、高端汽车的零配件达到1万余吨以上，运输微软等公司的电子产品超过了1.1万吨。郑州新

Airport to transform from a regional airport into an integrated transportation hub with global connectivity. Zhengzhou is becoming increasingly prominent as an aviation hub among the Belt and Road countries.

Zhengzhou has become the most important base of Cargolux Airlines International in the Asia-Pacific region and the fastest growing site in the global business. It is the company's distribution center and distribution base in Asia.

Zhengzhou Xinzheng International Airport continues to be the number one airport in terms of passenger and cargo volume in central China. In 2018, there were 44 passenger airlines operating at Zhengzhou Airport, with 187 passenger routes, 200,000 flights and 116 navigable points. There are 21 cargo airlines operating in Zhengzhou Airport, and 34 all-cargo flight routes have been opened. Zhengzhou Xinzheng International Airport has opened 16 flight points among the top 20 cargo hub airports in the world. There are 151 freight forwarding enterprises, among which 9 of the world's top 10 freight forwarding enterprises have been operating in Zhengzhou Xinzheng International Airport. It ranks the fourth only to Beijing, Shanghai and Guangzhou in the number of international freighter routes, flights and cargo volume.

Table: take-offs and landings of passenger, freight and flight at Zhengzhou Xinzheng International Airport

	2014	2015	2016	2017	2018	2019
Passenger capacity (million)	15.805	17.297	20.763	24.30	27.33	29.129
Cargo capacity (tons)	370,400	403,300	456,700	502,700	515,000	522,000
Total take-offs and landings	147,700	154,500	178,100	195,700	209,600	216,500

Source: "Aerotropolis in China: Zhengzhou Airport Economy Zone"

Zhengzhou Xinzheng International Airport service standard has become a benchmark to lead the development of the industry. As of April 2020, Zhengzhou Xinzheng International Airport has the function of seven major ports, namely,

郑国际机场与Inditex集团合作，在国内打造除上海之外的第二大物流分拨基地，同时也成为UPS公司在中国的第三大快件中心。

专栏：河南"空中丝绸之路"的"飞常"旅客——智利车厘子

中国是智利的第一大贸易伙伴，智利是中国第二大水果进口国。两国97%的商品实现了零关税。

智利南部盛产车厘子，每年11月至次年2月是车厘子成熟上市的季节，与中国正好存在一个生长周期时间差。中国是智利车厘子重要的海外销售市场。

在圣地亚哥附近的车厘子种植园被采摘后，一颗颗小小的车厘子开始了飞赴万里之外的中国旅行。以前如果是通过客货混装的飞机，它需要100多个小时才能达到目的地。如今，通过河南"空中丝绸之路"上的车厘子包机，它在经停欧洲后也只需要20多小时就能飞抵郑州，随后很快就会被分拨到北京、上海、广州等地，进入中国百姓的家庭。

据统计，智利对中国出口车厘子增长迅猛，出口额从2006年的100万美元增长到2018年的10亿美元。2018年，智利对中国出口的车厘子总量达到18万吨，占当年智利车厘子出口总量的88%。在智利对中国出口的车厘子中，约70%是由郑州机场口岸进境的。

2018年，河南"空中丝绸之路"智利圣地亚哥—郑州航线执飞了4架水果包机，全部由卢森堡货航完成；2019年，全年共有24架水果包机，其中8架的合作航空公司为卢森堡货航，16架的合作航空公司是康尼航空公司。

"中国市场一直在扩大，品质要求越来越高，我们也在不断调整品种。"智利纳提瓦车厘子种植园出口负责人巴勃罗·莫拉

fruit import port, frozen aquatic products import port, edible aquatic animal import port, meat import port, live animals import port, international mail hub port, and imported pharmaceuticals port, which makes it China's inland airport with the largest number of ports, and China's largest air-imported fruit distribution center. In order to improve the efficiency of international freight import and export customs clearance, Zhengzhou Xinzheng International Airport is equipped with a bonded area and a single-window electronic customs declaration and clearance system. The "1210" customs supervision mode of Zhengzhou has become a template for China's cross-border e-commerce. The coverage rate of customs declaration in the whole province has reached more than 90%, which marks the beginning of full implementation of 7×24-hour passenger and freight clearance. Zhengzhou Xinzheng International Airport has become an important distribution center for products of Germany's Daimler AG, BMW, high-end auto parts, as well as Microsoft, Lenovo and other electronic products. In 2018, the spare parts for Daimler AG, BMW and high-end cars of Germany reached more than 10,000 tons, and the electronic products of Microsoft and other companies transported reached more than 11,000 tons. Zhengzhou Xinzheng International Airport has cooperated with Inditex Group to build the second largest logistics distribution base in China after Shanghai, and has also become the third largest express delivery center of UPS in China.

Column: "Frequent Freight" of Henan's "Silk Road in the Air"— Cherries from Chile

China is Chile's largest trading partner, and Chile is China's second-largest fruit importer. The two countries have achieved zero tariffs on 97 percent of their goods.

The south of Chile is rich in cherries. From November to February of the following year is the season of ripe cherries, which makes a time difference with the growth cycle in China. China is an important overseas market for Chilean cherries.

After being picked at a cherry plantation near the Chilean capital Santiago, cherries set off on a journey thousands of miles into China. They

> 雷斯对中国市场的发展前景始终持乐观而坚定的评价。河南"空中丝绸之路"让中国与智利两国之间的联系愈发紧密。

在航空运输和物流领域内,河南"空中丝绸之路"具有强大的催化功能。2017年至今,成都、西安、兰州等多个城市先后提出发展本地的"空中丝绸之路"规划构想或实施方案。河南势必将与中国其他省市区

used to take more than 100 hours to reach their destination on a mixed cargo and passenger plane. Today, a cherry charter flight on the "Silk Road in the Air" in Henan Province takes just over 20 hours to reach Zhengzhou after stopping in Europe, after which the produce will be diverted to Beijing, Shanghai, Guangzhou and other places to enter the households of Chinese people.

Statistics show that Chile's exports of cherries to China have grown rapidly, from 1 million U.S. dollars in 2006 to 1 billion U.S. dollars in 2018. In 2018, Chile's total export of cherries to China reached 180,000 tons, accounting for 88 percent of Chile's total export of cherries that year. About 70 percent of Chile's cherries exported to China enter the country through Zhengzhou Airport.

In 2018, four fruit charter flights were carried out on the Santiago-Zhengzhou route of Henan's "Silk Road in the Air", all by Cargolux Airlines International. In 2019, there were 24 fruit charter flights, of which 8 were operated by Cargolux Airlines International and 16 by Coney Air.

"The Chinese market has been expanding, quality requirements are getting higher, and we are constantly adjusting our product varieties," said Pablo Molarez, head of exports at Chile's Nativa cherry plantation, who remained unwaveringly optimistic about the prospects for the Chinese market. China and Chile are more closely linked by Henan's "Silk Road in the Air".

In the field of air transport and logistics, Henan's "Silk Road in the Air" is highly catalytic. Since 2017, Chengdu, Xi'an, Lanzhou and other cities have put forward or implemented plans for the development of the "Silk Road in the Air". Henan will soon work with other provinces and regions in China to build China's "Silk Road in the Air".

In 2018, China Civil Aviation Administration and the Government of Henan Province jointly formulated *The Strategic Plan for Zhengzhou's International Air Cargo Hub*. This is China's only cargo-based airport strategic planning. In the future, the strategic goal of Zhengzhou Xinzheng International Airport is to become "a global air cargo hub, a modern international comprehensive

一起努力融合,共同搭建中国"空中丝绸之路"。

2018年,中国民用航空局与河南省人民政府联合编制了《郑州国际航空货运枢纽战略规划》。这是中国唯一以货运为主的机场战略规划。今后郑州新郑国际机场的战略目标是成为"全球航空货运枢纽、现代国际综合交通枢纽、航空物流改革创新试验区和中部崛起的新动力源"。同一时期,国务院《关于支持自由贸易实验区深化改革创新若干措施的通知》明确提出,在对外航权谈判中支持郑州机场利用第五航权,在平等互利的基础上允许外国航空公司承载经郑州至第三国的客货业务,积极向国外航空公司推荐并引导申请加入中国市场的国外航空公司执飞郑州机场。河南"空中丝绸之路"的未来有着更令人期待的发展愿景。

transportation hub, a pilot area for aviation logistics reform and innovation, and a new power source for the rise of central China". At the same time, the State Council issued *The Notice of Support for Free Trade Area's Deepening Reform and Innovation Measures*, allowing foreign airlines to carry passenger and cargo business via Zhengzhou to third countries, observing the Fifth Freedom and actively recommending foreign airlines to join the Chinese market through Zhengzhou Airport on the basis of equality and mutual benefit, therefore the "Silk Road in the Air" in Henan has a brighter future.

二、河南"空中丝绸之路"产业集聚效应突出,推动了河南省地方经济社会高质量发展

航空运输在空间内具有自我增强机制的聚集效应,能够以机场为中心引致相关产业形成特定的产业集群。河南"空中丝绸之路"在天空中用洲际航线编织出蓝图,同时也在地面上促成新兴产业在郑州落地发展。郑州航空港经济综合实验区成为河南"空中丝绸之路"的最重要空间载体。

自2013年以来,作为中国首个国家级航空港经济实验区,郑州航空港经济综合实验区与河南"空中丝绸之路"密切互动,跨境电商、智能终端(手机)、高端制造以及生物医药等行业相继入驻实验区,实现了产业空间集聚,完善了产业环节链条,优化了产业结构模式。

1. 跨境电商业迅速崛起

河南省的跨境电商进出口规模在全国位居前列。2018年,河南跨境电商进出口交易额1289.2亿元,全省累计创建了2个国家级电子商务示范城市、3个国家级示范基地和6个国家级示范企业。

作为河南"空中丝绸之路"枢纽之一,郑州在2018年跨境电商进、出口清单合计9507.3万票,进出口商品总值120.4亿元,在全国跨境电商零售进出口交易额排名第四位。《中国航空经济发展指数报告(2019)》显示,2018年,在全国36个航空经济区发展评比中,郑州的体制机制创新指数排名第四。

郑州航空港经济综合实验区在中国(郑州)跨境电子商务综合试验区中具有创新龙头带动作用。2018年,郑州航空港经济综合实验区跨境电商零售进出口完成2114.36万单,实现货值23.78亿元;2019年继续保持增长态势,进出口单数和货值分别增长244.79%和196.85%,总量在

II. The Agglomeration Effect of Henan's "Silk Road in the Air" in Pushing Henan's Local Economy to the Level of High-quality Development

The construction of an air transport hub can lead to the formation of specific industrial clusters with the airport as the center. Henan's "Silk Road in the Air" blueprint for intercontinental air freight facilitates the development of new industries on the ground in Zhengzhou. The Zhengzhou Airport Comprehensive Economic Experimental Area has become the strategic center of the "Silk Road in the Air" in Henan Province.

Since 2013, as China's first national airport economy zone, the Zhengzhou Airport Comprehensive Economic Experimental Area has actively interacted with the "Silk Road in the Air" project in Henan. Cross-border E-commerce, intelligent mobile phone terminals, high-tech manufacturing and the biomedicine industry established their bases one after another in the experimental area, improving the links of the industrial chain and optimizing the industrial structure.

1. The Rapid Rise of Cross-border E-commerce

The import and export volume of cross-border E-commerce in Henan Province ranks among the highest ones in China. In 2018, the import and export volume of cross-border E-commerce in Henan reached 128.92 billion Yuan, and Henan Province has set up two national-level E-commerce demonstration cities, three national-level demonstration bases and six national-level demonstration enterprises.

As one of the hubs of Henan's "Silk Road in the Air", Zhengzhou received 95.073 million cross-border E-commerce import and export lists in 2018 with a total import and export value of 12.04 billion Yuan, ranking fourth in China's cross-border E-commerce retail import and export volume. According to *The Report on China's Airport Economic Development Index (2019)*, Zhengzhou ranked fourth in the institutional innovation index among 36 airport economic areas in China in 2018.

The Zhengzhou Airport Economic Zone plays an innovative leading role in

郑州跨境电商综合试验区的占比已超过50%。截至2019年底，在郑州航空港经济综合实验区备案或注册的电商企业有720家，其中入驻郑州新郑国际机场的物流企业超过100家，引进顺丰、申通、菜鸟网络、苏宁等30多个物流项目，年营业收入70余亿元，全年跨境电商单量日均稳定在6万单左右，形成了包括电商平台、仓储、物流、关务、结算企业在内的跨境产业链，跨境电商产业集聚效应不断显现，郑州航空港经济综合实验区成为国内外知名电商的汇集地。郑州作为物流枢纽中心，来自全球的货物经由国际航班运抵后，马上就会被派往全国；同时，中原地

the China (Zhengzhou) cross-border E-commerce Comprehensive Experimental Area. In 2018, import and export of cross-border E-commerce in the airport trade area reached 21.1436 million orders, with a value of 2.378 billion Yuan. In 2019, the number of imports and exports and the value of goods increased by 244.79% and 196.85% respectively, accounting for more than 50% of the total cross-border E-commerce in Zhengzhou. By the end of 2019, 720 E-commerce enterprises had registered in the cross-border E-commerce Comprehensive Experimental Area. More than 100 logistics enterprises registered in Zhengzhou Xinzheng International Airport, including more than 30 logistics networks such as S.F. Express, STO Express, CAINIAO Logistic Network and Suning Logistic, with an operating income of more than 7 billion Yuan, and an average daily cross-border E-commerce volume of about 60,000, helping to build an E-commerce chain of electronic business platforms, warehousing, logistics, customs affairs solutions and settlement. Zhengzhou Airport has become a domestic and cross-border E-commerce headquarters. As a logistics hub, Zhengzhou will introduce goods from all over the world to China as soon as they arrive via international flights. At the same time, the featured commodities, high-tech manufacture and high value-added agricultural and sideline products of the central plain regions have also been efficiently distributed to all parts of the world. The logistics and transportation mode of "transport + distribution" has brought vitality to cross-border E-commerce.

During the COVID-19 epidemic period in early 2020, the air cargo of Henan's "Silk Road in the Air" played a strategic supporting role in the fight against the epidemic and in the economic and social development.

> **Column: Henan's "Silk Road in the Air" under COVID-19 Epidemic**
> During the global outbreak of COVID-19, Cargolux Airlines International and Air Longhao Airlines Co., Ltd. coordinated cargo carriers to ensure the transportation of epidemic relief supplies and other imported and exported goods.
> On February 14, 2020, Cargolux Airlines International resumed flights between Zhengzhou and Luxembourg. About 24 tons of epidemic relief

区的特色商品、高端制造业和高附加值农副产品也被迅速装运飞往世界各地的航班。"运+派"的物流运输模式使得跨境电商迸发出积极的活力。

2020年初，新冠肺炎疫情在全球爆发。在疫情期间，河南"空中丝绸之路"发挥出航空货运在抗击疫情和经济社会发展中的战略支撑作用。

> **专栏：新冠肺炎疫情下的河南"空中丝绸之路"**
>
> 在全球疫情爆发期间，卢森堡货航和中原龙浩航空有限公司发挥"一外一内"双货航协同优势，全力确保了防疫救援物资和进出口货物的运输工作。
>
> 2020年2月14日，卢森堡货航恢复了郑州—卢森堡航线航班。通过加开郑州—大阪—武汉包机航线，为湖北义务运送海外捐助口罩、防护服、护目镜等防疫物资约24吨。中原龙浩航空公司打通了河内—郑州航空物流通道，成为国内第一家恢复运营中越国际货运航线的航空公司，加密郑州—合肥—河内航线每周至7班。组建抗疫志愿者小组，为世界各地捐赠者"免费带货"，累计协助20多个国家的捐赠者将约300万件防疫物资顺利运抵以武汉为主的抗疫一线城市。面对货源企业复工推迟等困难，为国内各厂商、贸易企业从欧洲带回所需汽车零配件、电子元件等生产物料；同时，保障河南及周边地区的复产企业产品运往欧洲。
>
> 河南也大力支持卢森堡国内疫情的防控工作。2020年3月22日，河南省为卢森堡紧急筹措的首批总价值超过250万元的医疗物资直接运抵卢森堡。
>
> 2020年1月1日至4月17日，河南"空中丝绸之路"卢森堡国际航空货运公司累计执飞137班，货运量约2.04万吨；中原龙浩航空有限公司累计执飞529班，货运量约4209吨。

supplies such as masks, protective clothing and goggles were delivered to Hubei Province for free by additional charter flights on the Zhengzhou-Osaka-Wuhan air route. China Central Longhao Airlines Co., Ltd. opened the logistics channel between Hanoi and Zhengzhou, being the first airline in China to resume the operation of Sino Vietnam International cargo routes, and the Zhengzhou-Hefei-Hanoi routes are encrypted to 7 flights per week. A volunteer team was set up to transport donated supplies from around the world, and helped donors from more than 20 countries deliver about 3 million medical relief items to the epidemic centers, such as Wuhan. During the recovery period, Henan's "Silk Road in the Air" has brought production materials such as auto parts and electronic components from Europe for domestic manufacturers and trading enterprises in order to facilitate the resumption of work. At the same time, it has ensured that products from Henan and its neighboring provinces are shipped to Europe.

Henan also aided the control and prevention of the epidemic in Luxembourg. On March 22, 2020, the first batch of medical supplies, with a total value of more than 2.5 million Yuan, raised by Henan Province, was delivered directly to Luxembourg.

From January 1 to April 17, 2020, Cargolux Airlines International carried out a total of 137 flights along Henan's "Silk Road in the Air", carrying about 20,400 tons of cargo. Air Longhao Airlines Co., Ltd. has operated 529 flights with a cargo volume of about 4,209 tons.

On June 14, 2020, the Prime Minister of Luxembourg Bettel delivered a video speech at the "Silk Road in the Air" symposium in Henan Province, praising the role of the "Silk Road in the Air" in Henan Province. "A world-class air logistics ecosystem is emerging," he said. "During the epidemic period, the "Silk Road in the Air"' became an important lifeline for Luxembourg and other parts of Europe. It was a bridge in need in the air."

To build an international air cargo hub, Henan needs to perfect its ground service and customs clearance environment.

In order to better protect the international logistics business, Zhengzhou

> 2020年6月14日，在河南省"空中丝绸之路"座谈会上，卢森堡首相贝泰尔发表了视频致辞，高度评价了河南"空中丝绸之路"的作用。他认为"（双方）通力合作、集思广益，一个世界级的空中物流生态正在崛起；在疫情期间，'空中丝绸之路'已成为卢森堡及其他欧洲地区的'重要生命线'，这是一条雪中送炭的'空中桥梁'"。

打造国际航空货运枢纽离不开完善的地面服务和便利的通关环境等因素的支撑。

为更好地保障国际物流业务，郑州新郑国际机场研发使用多式联运数据交易服务平台，初步实现了郑州—卢森堡、郑州—芝加哥两条专线的在线订舱、境内外卡车在线约车和物流信息全程追踪等服务。该平台是国内唯一一家以机场为中心搭建的智能化平台，与河南保税物流中心、陆港公司、大连港以及国内外卡车公司等初步实现信息互联互通。同时，郑州新郑国际机场还发起成立"国际物流数据标准"联盟，与国泰航空、Forward Air、新起点等航空公司和货代企业完成物流跟踪数据对接，形成了航空物流大数据共享。

河南还创新设计了跨境电商保税备货模式。在郑州中大门国际购物公园，顾客可以实现跨境O2O自提，收货时间由原来的半个月时间间隔缩短到3分钟，顾客在家门口可以购买来自全球70多个国家和地区的10万多种商品，商品品质实现全程可追溯。

2. 航空产业链核心业务不断完善

河南"空中丝绸之路"带动了本省航空全产业链骨架网络建设，航空租赁、航空培训等一系列关联行业项目的落地填补了河南省产业空白，为河南"空中丝绸之路"注入了全新动力。

Xinzheng International Airport is developing a transport data transaction service platform, which coordinates the online booking of domestic and foreign trucks as well as logistics information tracking and other services for the two special Zhengzhou-Luxembourg-Chicago lines. The intelligent platform integrates information from the Henan Bonded Logistics Center, Inland Port Company, Dalian Harbor and domestic and foreign truck companies. At the same time, Zhengzhou Xinzheng International Airport also established the "International Logistics Data Standard" Alliance, and implemented logistics tracking data sharing via aligned channels with airlines such as Cathay Pacific Airways, Forward Air, New Start Company and freight forwarding enterprises, forming an aviation logistics big data sharing system.

Henan also improved the design of the cross-border E-commerce bonded stock mode. In Zhengzhou Central Gate International Shopping Park, customers can select their O2O cross-border orders by themselves. The time of receiving goods is shortened from half a month to 3 minutes. Customers can buy more than 100,000 kinds of goods from more than 70 countries and regions at home whose quality can be wholly traced.

2. The Core Business of the Aviation Industry Chain Is Continuously Improved

The "Silk Road in the Air" has set up a whole framework around the aviation industry in Henan Province. A series of related industrial projects, such as aviation leasing and aviation training, have filled the industrial gap in Henan Province and injected new impetus into its economic initiatives.

(1) The Breakthrough in the Aircraft Leasing Industry

In 2016, Henan Civil Aviation Development and Investment Co., Ltd. and Lithuania AviaAM Leasing Group established Avia Financial Leasing (China) Co., Ltd., realizing the breakthrough of the aircraft leasing industry in Henan. On December 8, 2016, the international leasing of 16 aircraft, at a value of 801 million U.S. dollars, was completed on the day of the company's opening ceremony. The completion of this business is regarded as a grand gesture of "opening up to the world and achieving win-win results", and is an example of Henan "developing in harmony with the world economy".

（1）飞机租赁业实现破局发展

2016年，河南航投与立陶宛AviaAM租赁集团成立了阿维亚融资租赁（中国）有限公司，实现了河南航空业飞机租赁业零的突破，结束了河南没有飞机租赁业态的历史。同年12月8日，在公司揭牌当日即完成了16架飞机租赁的国际业务，涉及金额8.01亿美元。此笔业务的完成被视为"对外开放、优势互补、多方共赢"的大手笔，是"走出去与世界经济相融发展"的生动案例。

2017年，阿维亚融资租赁（中国）有限公司在短短5个月时间里交付了8架飞机，提前3个月完成了全年任务。2018年，阿维亚融资租赁（中国）有限公司突破传统飞机租赁业务模式，首次在境外公海区域完成交付的跨境、跨区转租赁业务，在购买、支付、入关、税收等方面大幅优化了交易结构，有效解决了资产转让方、飞机制造商、承租方面临的各种问题，实现交易多方利益最大化。公司荣膺全球最有影响力航空金融杂志之一*Airline Economics*（《航空经济》）颁发的"亚太区年度最佳融资交易奖"。同年10月，内资航空设备租赁公司——河南航投航空设备租赁有限公司成立，并在郑州航空港经济综合实验区交付1架B737-800到岸飞机。

2019年，阿维亚融资租赁（中国）有限公司加快机队组合的扩张，着力推动客户多元化发展。同年5月16日，公司完成首笔附带租约的飞机资产交易，通过购买孤儿信托受益权的方式，打通了境外航空金融市场的融资渠道，将一家B777宽体客机承租给阿联酋航空。12月31日，公司完成首单境内飞机资产包交易。

与飞机租赁业务密切相关的SPV公司相继在郑州航空港经济综合实验区（郑州新郑综合保税区）注册成立，2019年，注册成立的飞机租赁SPV公司已经达到20家，累计完成5架租赁飞机交付及3单飞机资产包业务，运营飞机资产共计4.5亿美元。

In 2017, Avia Financial Leasing (China) Co., Ltd. delivered eight aircraft in just five months, completing the annual mission three months ahead of schedule. In 2018, Avia Financing Leasing (China) Co., Ltd. broke out of the traditional model of the aircraft leasing business, and delivered the cross-border inter-district leasing business, and optimized trade structure in purchase, payment, customs and tax. The new business model effectively solved problems relating to the assets of the assigning party, aircraft manufacturers and tenants, thereby maximizing trading interests. The company was named the "Best Financing Award in the Asia-Pacific Region" by *Airline Economics*, one of the world's most influential aviation finance magazines. In October 2018, Henan Civil Aviation Development and Investment Equipment Leasing Co., Ltd., a domestic aviation equipment leasing company, was established, and delivered one B737-800 plane to the Zhengzhou Airport Economic Zone.

In 2019, Avia Financial Leasing (China) Co., Ltd. accelerated the expansion of its fleet portfolio to promote diversified development. On May 16, 2019, the company completed the first aircraft asset transaction with lease attached, and through the purchase of beneficial rights of the orphan trust, it opened up a financing channel with the overseas aviation financial market and leased a B777 plane to Emirates Airlines. On December 31, the company completed the first domestic aircraft asset package transaction.

SPV companies related to the aircraft leasing business were registered in the Zhengzhou Airport Economic Zone. The number of registered aircraft leasing SPV companies reached 20 in 2019. A total of 5 aircraft leasing deliveries and 3 individual aircraft asset packs were completed, totaling 450 million U.S. dollars.

(2) Aviation Training and Education Gets Started

On July 29, 2019, ASG Group and Henan Civil Aviation Development and Investment Co., Ltd. signed an agreement to co-fund a new joint venture, BAA Training China Co., Ltd., which will function as a training center in Zhengzhou. The construction of the training center began on October 25. After its completion, the center will provide pilot and flight attendant training services to airlines and other users, being the first professional training institution of its kind in Henan Province. At the beginning of the project, six full-automatic flight simulators will be introduced, and it is estimated that 4,000 pilots will be trained each year. In

(2)航空培训教育开始起步

2019年7月29日,阿维亚解决方案集团(ASG Group)与河南航投签署合资合作协议,双方设立新合资公司BAA培训中国公司(BAA Training China Co.,Ltd),在郑州运营商用飞机航空培训中心。10月25日,培训中心开工建设。建成后将向航空公司等用户提供飞行员、乘务员训练服务,从而填补了河南省没有专业飞行员培训机构的空白。项目初期将引入6台全自动飞行模拟器,预计每年培训飞行员4000名。项目中期将围绕打造民航培训全产业链,开展航材库、乘务培训、机务培训、应急生存训练、空保培训、航务培训等项目。立陶宛外交部前部长、阿维亚董事维格达斯表示,"BAA(中国)航空培训中心将成为河南航投和阿维亚紧密强劲关系的新基石"。

与此同时,河南整合本省航空教育、飞行培训方面的优势资源,依托本地优势资源组建飞行培训学院。2020年4月23日,河南航投与安阳市政府、安阳工学院签署合作协议,在安阳设立民航141部国际飞行学院,为"空中丝绸之路"建设提供人才支撑。

3. 智能终端产业集聚效应日趋凸显

2010年,富士康科技集团在郑州投资建厂,为日后的智能终端产业奠定了基础。随后,中兴、大神、年富、商贸通等208个相关项目先后入驻,从芯片、面板到整机,从硬件到软件的全产业链布局逐步形成。2017年,郑州航空港经济综合实验区内企业生产的手机总量达到2.99亿部,其中苹果手机产量约1亿部,基本确立了全球智能终端(手机)生产基地的地位。

2020年3月17日,投资12亿元的几米物联网智能终端生产基地及总部研发项目正式确定落户郑州航空港经济综合实验区。该项目是郑州航空港经济综合实验区智能终端产业的首个总部型项目,填补了郑州航空港经济综合实验区智能终端(手机)产业园高端制造业的空白,推动了

the middle stage, the whole industry chain of civil aviation training is expected to be conducted, and such projects as aviation material warehouse building, crew training, cabin service training, emergency survival training, air maintenance training and aviation operation training will be carried out. Former Minister of Foreign Affairs of Lithuania and Avia Director Vigdas stated that "BAA (China) Aviation Training Center will become a new cornerstone of the close and strong relationship between Avia and Henan Civil Aviation Development and Investment Co., Ltd."

At the same time, by taking advantages of its local resources in aviation education and flight training, Henan has established a flight training college. On April 23, 2020, Henan Civil Aviation Development and Investment Co., Ltd. signed a cooperation agreement with Anyang Municipal Government and Anyang Institute of Technology to set up an international flight college—Civil Aviation Department 141—in Anyang, providing talent support for the construction of the "Silk Road in the Air".

3. The Agglomeration Effect of the Intelligent Terminal Industry Has Become More Obvious

In 2010, Foxconn Technology Group built a factory in Zhengzhou, laying the foundation for the future intelligent terminal industry. Subsequently, 208 related projects such as ZTE, Dazen, Nianfu and Trade Link were successively settled here, and the whole industrial chain layout from chips, panels to complete machines, from hardware to software was gradually formed. In 2017, the total number of mobile phones produced by enterprises in Zhengzhou Airport Economic Zone reached 299 million, including 100 million iPhones, establishing the zone as a global production base of smart terminals (mobile phones).

On March 17, 2020, Jimi Group invested 1.2 billion yuan to settle its intelligent terminal production base and R&D project headquarters in the Airport Economic Zone. This project is the first headquarters project of the intelligent terminal industry in this region, which fills a gap in the high-end manufacturing sector in the Zhengzhou Airport Economic Zone. The project promotes the transition from the traditional manufacturing industry to the advanced manufacturing and modern service industries.

园区企业由传统制造业向先进制造业和现代服务业的深度融合转型。

截至2020年4月，智能终端（手机）产业园已经有联创电子、领胜科技、华讯方舟等75家企业入驻，投产非苹果智能终端企业38家，年产手机超过1亿部。产业园成为河南智能终端产业走向全球的窗口。

4. 电子信息先进制造业发展取得实效

智能终端（手机）企业在郑州航空港经济综合实验区的集聚式发展产生了传导促进作用，带动了芯片、面板等半导体生产制造业项目落地。

2017年7月27日，年产240万片200毫米单晶硅抛光片项目在郑州航空港经济综合实验区投产。该项目是河南省首个单晶硅片生产项目，填补了河南半导体集成电路基础材料行业的空白，对于推动郑州航空港经济综合实验区打造世界级电子信息先进制造业集群，推进半导体集成电路产业加快发展，重塑电子信息产业发展新格局具有重要意义。

2018年，河南省第一条第5代TFT-LCD生产线及CF生产线在郑州航空港经济综合实验区建成投产，每年可生产一亿片（5寸）液晶显示面板。半导体封装划片机、DW先进集成电路芯片靶材等项目也先后在郑州航空港经济综合实验区投产。2018年，郑州航空港经济综合实验区电子信息业产值达到3084.2亿元。

5. 生物医药产业稳步发展

2017年，在政府和企业多方合作下，郑州临空生物医药园开园建设。通过依托郑州航空港经济综合实验区的区位优势，郑州临空生物医药园重点建设新药研发平台、小动物新药评价平台、小分子CMC制剂研发平台、大分子中试生产服务平台、细胞技术服务平台五大专业公共技术服务平台，创新药、IVD/第三方检测、细胞技术、医疗器械等为主要发展方向。

By April 2020, 75 enterprises such as Lianchuang Electronics, Lingsheng Technology, Huaxunchina, etc. were settled in the smart terminal (mobile phone) industrial park, and 38 non-Apple smart terminal enterprises had been put into production, with an annual output of more than 100 million mobile phones. The industrial park has become a window for Henan's intelligent terminal industry to go global.

4. The Development of the Advanced Electronic Information Manufacturing Industry Has Achieved Tangible Results

The development of intelligent terminal (mobile phone) enterprises in the Zhengzhou Airport Economic Zone has played a pivotal role in the implementation of semiconductor manufacturing projects such as chips and panels.

On July 27, 2017, the project, with an annual output of 2.4 million 200 mm mono-crystalline silicon polished pieces, was put into operation in the Zhengzhou Airport Economic Zone. The project is the first of its type in Henan Province, and has been of great significance for promoting the Airport Economic Zone as a world-class advanced electronic information manufacturing industry cluster, speeding up the development of semiconductor integrated circuit industry and reshaping the development of the electronic information industry.

In 2018, the first fifth-generation TFT-LCD production line and CF production line of Henan Province were put into operation in the Airport Economic Zone, which can produce 100 million (5-inch) liquid crystal display panels every year. Semiconductor packaging and dicing machine, DW advanced integrated circuit chip target material and other projects have also been put into production in the Airport Economic Zone. In 2018, the electronic information industry output value of Zhengzhou Airport Economic Zone reached 308.42 billion yuan.

5. The Biomedical Industry Has Been Developing Steadily

In 2017, as a cooperative initiative between the government and local enterprises, Zhengzhou Linkong Biomedical Park was constructed. Relying on the regional advantage of the Airport Economic Zone, Zhengzhou Linkong Biomedical Park constructed five professional public technology service platforms: a

截至2018年年末，生物医药产业园区已吸引了70余家生物医药企业签约入驻，涵盖化学药物、细胞治疗、诊断试剂、医药物流等领域，总产值近5亿元。

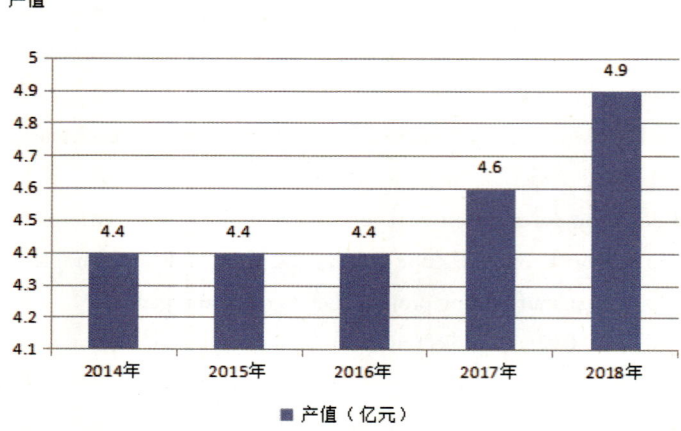

郑州航空港经济综合实验区生物医药行业产值

银行类以及保险公司、信托投资公司、基金投资管理公司等非银行类金融机构先后入驻郑州航空公司经济综合实验区。截至2018年底，入驻实验区行业银行分支机构20家、保险业金融机构8家。同时，为适应区内跨国公司离岸金融需求，区域性离岸金融中心的建设也正在提速。

在"空中丝绸之路"合作形成后，河南省与卢森堡"一带一路"经济合作论坛形成了双年交替举办常态化机制，卢森堡金融推广署也定期在郑州举行金融推介会，河南省与卢森堡两地之间的金融合作领域日渐增大。

new drug research and development platform, a small animals new drug evaluation platform, a micromolecule CMC preparation research and development platform, a macromolecule pilot production research and development platform, and a cell technology service platform. This project focuses on innovative medicine, IVD or third party detection, cell technology and medical equipment.

By the end of 2018, the biomedical industrial park had embraced more than 70 biomedical enterprises, covering chemical drugs, cell therapy, diagnostic reagents, pharmaceutical logistics and other fields, with a total output value of nearly 500 million yuan.

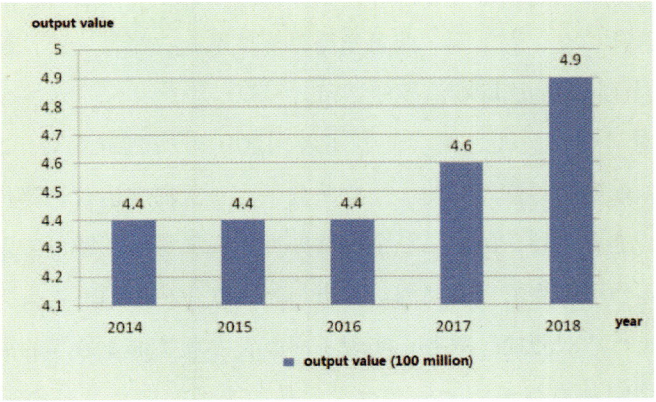

The output value of biomedical industry in Zhengzhou Airport Economy Zone

Many banks, insurance companies, trust investment companies, fund investment management companies and other non-bank financial institutions have settled in the Zhengzhou Airport Economy Zone. By the end of 2018, 20 bank branches and 8 insurance institutions had settled in the Zone. In order to meet the offshore financial needs of multinational companies in the region, the construction of regional offshore financial centers is speeding up.

Following their "Silk Road in the Air" cooperation, Henan Province and Luxembourg instituted a biennial Belt and Road Initiative Economic Cooperation Forum, Luxembourg's Financial Promotion Agency has held regular financial promotion meetings in Zhengzhou, and as a result, financial cooperation between Henan Province and Luxembourg is growing.

三、河南"空中丝绸之路"人文交流效应突出,促进了中外旅游历史交流互动

河南"空中丝绸之路"的建设吸引着全球的注意力,通过宣传河南"空中丝绸之路",也向全球展示了河南创新进取的形象。2019年,中国国家主席习近平访问法国期间,法国发行量最大和最具影响力的报纸《费加罗报》刊登文章《中国郑州:"国际商都"城市启航》介绍郑州通过打造陆、空、海、网"四条丝路"深度融入"一带一路"建设,成为中国内地新型的国际物流枢纽城市。

河南"空中丝绸之路"便利了各国居民开展旅游活动。2018年4月,卢森堡旅游签证(郑州)便捷服务平台正式揭牌运营,郑州市成为除北京、上海之外,国内第三个能够办理卢森堡签证的城市。该平台的成立与运作可以为河南省及周边省市与26个欧盟申根国家人员交往提供签证、出行"双便捷"服务,实现了河南省办理签证业务零的突破。近年来,中国赴卢森堡旅游的游客已经从原来的寥寥无几状态上升到每年超过15万人次,卢森堡人学习中文的热情也空前高涨。2019年5月至6月,卢森堡旅游签证(郑州)便捷服务平台还连续举办了两场英国"如意签"活动,为暑期青少年夏令营、旅游团办理英国签证。

> **专栏:在家门口办理赴欧旅行签证**
>
> 2016年10月起,中国游客办理欧洲申根国家签证时必须到相应国家的领事馆进行指纹采集。通常,河南省的旅客办理欧洲申根国家签证需要到北京、上海等城市录取指纹。
>
> 2017年6月,根据中卢双方签署的协议,卢森堡驻中国大使馆开始在卢森堡旅游签证(郑州)便捷服务平台为中国居民办理签

III. The Promotion of Tourism and Cultural Exchanges between China and Foreign Countries

Henan's "Silk Road in the Air" demonstrates Henan's innovative and enterprising spirit to the most world. In 2019, when Chinese President Xi Jinping paid a visit to France, the most influential French newspaper *Le Figaro* published the article "China Zhengzhou, an International Business City, Setting Sail". The article introduced Zhengzhou's integration into the Belt and Road Initiative through building "four silk roads": air, land, sea and internet, and that Zhengzhou has become an international logistics hub in China's mainland.

In April 2018, the Luxembourg Tourist Visa (Zhengzhou) Convenient Service Platform was officially launched and put into operation, making it easier for international visitors to travel to Henan Province. Zhengzhou became the third city in China, after Beijing and Shanghai, to enable people to apply for a Luxembourg visa. The establishment and operation of the platform provides convenient services for people in Henan and surrounding provinces. People from 26 EU Schengen countries can apply for visas and travel in Henan Province. In recent years, the number of Chinese tourists to Luxembourg has increased from a small number to more than 150,000 each year, and the enthusiasm of Luxembourgers to learn Chinese has never been higher. In May and June 2019, the Luxembourg Tourist Visa (Zhengzhou) Convenient Service Platform held two consecutive activities to apply for UK visas for youth summer camps and tour groups.

Column: Applying for a Europe Travel Visa at Home

Starting from October 2016, Chinese tourists must go to the consulate of the corresponding country for fingerprint collection when applying for a visa to a European Schengen country. Travelers from Henan Province previously needed to go to Beijing or Shanghai to apply for a European Schengen visa.

In June 2017, in accordance with the agreement signed between

证便利业务。卢森堡驻华使馆在郑州为河南及周边居民提供个人信息采集服务；中国申请签证者可以在郑州递交申根签证申请材料和生物信息采集工作，然后在2—3个工作日就可拿到签证，实现畅游申根26国。与原来专门赴北京申请签证相比，此举可以为河南百姓节约人均1500元左右的费用和7个工作日的时间。

卢森堡旅游签证（郑州）便捷服务平台还提供配套服务，如申根签证咨询及表格协助，帮助申请人完成在线表格申请；核查申请人有关资料；以及欧洲旅游产品咨询，保险代买，机票、酒店代订等多项内容。

签证服务平台的运营将进一步提升郑州国家中心城市的竞争力、辐射力、影响力，在河南"空中丝绸之路"货运积累基础上，增加人文交流。

河南"空中丝绸之路"搭建起历史文化传播桥梁。自古以来，河南与"丝绸之路"沿线国家保持着密切联系。在东汉时期，洛阳是中西方"丝绸之路"的起点。中国的丝绸、漆器和铁器被传至中亚、西亚乃至地中海东岸地区，西域的骏马、狮子、鸵鸟和胡桃、苜蓿、葡萄和石榴等也被带入中原。印度佛教也是通过"丝绸之路"传入中原内地。在宋、元、明、清时期，随着海上丝绸之路日益繁盛，开封成为海上丝绸之路的目的地和出发地，中原地区的丝绸和瓷器通过水路运销世界各地。如今，河南又通过"空中丝绸之路"进一步加大与沿线国家的联系。河南先后派出50多个文化艺术团组在70多个国家和地区举办了各类文化活动400余场，连续举办了6届中国（郑州）国际旅游城市市长论坛。2018年11月，河南省博物院赴卢森堡举行"华夏文明之源——河南文物珍宝展"。偃师二里头遗址出土的青铜器及陶器、安阳殷墟出土的商代"妇好"方罍等140多件文物被运抵卢森堡国家历史与艺术博物

> China and Luxembourg, the embassy of Luxembourg began processing visa applications for Chinese residents using the Luxembourg Tourist Visa (Zhengzhou) Convenient Service Platform. The Luxembourg embassy in Zhengzhou provides personal information collection services for residents of Henan and its surrounding areas. Visa applicants can submit their Schengen visa application materials and collect biological information in Zhengzhou, and receive their visas in 2-3 working days. Compared with the former procedure, this can save Henan people about 1,500 yuan per person and seven working days.
>
> The Luxembourg Tourist Visa (Zhengzhou) Convenient Service Platform also provides support services, including Schengen visa consultation, online form filling assistance and applicant information verification, as well as European tourism product consultation, insurance purchase, air tickets and hotel booking and other services.
>
> The visa service platform will further enhance the competitiveness and influence of Zhengzhou as a central city, and increase cultural exchanges along the "Silk Road in the Air".

Henan's "Silk Road in the Air" has provided a bridge for the cultural transmission. Since ancient times, Henan has maintained close ties with countries along the "Silk Road". During the Eastern Han Dynasty, Luoyang was the starting point of the "Silk Road". Chinese silk, lacquerware, and ironware were spread to Central Asia, West Asia, and even the eastern coast of the Mediterranean. Horses, lions, ostriches, walnuts, alfalfa, grapes, and pomegranates from the Western Regions were also brought into the Central Plains. Indian Buddhism was also introduced into the Central Plains through the "Silk Road". During the Song, Yuan, Ming and Qing dynasties, as the Maritime Silk Road became increasingly prosperous, Kaifeng became the destination and departure point of the Maritime Silk Road. Silk and porcelain from the Central Plains were shipped to all parts of the world by water. Now, Henan has further increased its ties with countries along the "Silk Road in the Air". Henan has sent more than 50 cultural and art troupes to hold more than 400 cultural events in over 70

馆。展览从帝国形成和匠作技艺两部分再现华夏文明诞生、演变、发展的历史进程，展示中原大地自古形成的繁荣祥和、包容大气的物质与精神面貌，再现不同民族、不同文化在中原大地上相互尊重、彼此包容、共同发展的历史进程。展览引发了当地群众的极大观展热情，来自英国、法国、德国、荷兰和比利时等国的观众和华人华侨社团观众到馆参观。2018年11月22日至2019年4月末展出期间，累计接待观众人数超过9万人。

countries and regions, and has held China (Zhengzhou) International Tourism Cities' Mayors' Forum for six times. In November 2018, Henan Museum held an exhibition of Henan cultural relics and treasures in Luxembourg. More than 140 relics including bronzeware and pottery found in Erlitou Site of Yanshi, "fu hao fang jia" unearthed in the Yin Dynasty Ruins in Anyang, were exhibited in the Luxembourg National Museum of History and Art. The exhibition reproduced the emergence, evolution, and development of Chinese civilization, the prosperity of central China since the ancient times, and the historical period when different nationalities and cultures peacefully co-existed with each other. The exhibition aroused great enthusiasm among local people, and attracted visitors from Britain, France, Germany, Netherlands and Belgium, as well as the overseas Chinese community. During the exhibition (November 2018-April 2019), the cumulative audience exceeded 90,000.

四、河南"空中丝绸之路"带路引领效应突出,推动了中国与西方国家、南南国家双方向关系突破

"空中丝绸之路"强化了中国与欧洲等发达地区之间的融合度,改善和平衡了当前"一带一路"建设的空间格局。

卢森堡居于西欧的十字路口,具有独特的区位优势,可辐射至拥有约5亿消费者的整个欧洲市场,尤其是对周边的德国、法国、比利时等欧盟主要国家具有很强的辐射作用。据估算,欧盟40%的财富集中在卢森堡周边500千米范围之内。河南"空中丝绸之路"的搭建,使河南和卢森堡成为连接中国与欧洲的重要支点,促进了中国与欧盟可持续性、深层次经贸合作。

"空中丝绸之路"还进一步加深了南南国家合作。2019年4月底,"空中丝绸之路南南合作伙伴联盟"项目正式被列入第二届"一带一路"国际合作高峰论坛成果清单,并向全球进行发布。同年5月,该项目与第二届峰会成果清单一起被列入联合国工作清单。以此为契机,"全球南南发展博览会""空中丝绸之路南南合作基金"等一系列重大项目正在落实推进,努力成为中国与南南国家、地区和城市的文化交流平台、市场对接平台、产能合作平台,推进全方位、多层次、宽领域开放共享、互利共赢。

河南"空中丝绸之路"自开通以来,让河南省与全球200多个国家和地区建立起紧密的经贸往来,实现了商品、货物、人员、信息和资金等要素跨境流动,推动了河南省更加深入、广泛地参与全球的产业链、价值链、供应链体系。

河南"空中丝绸之路"的实践再次证明,航空运输业能够实现在全球范围内配置高端生产要素和促进地区跨越式发展,国际性航空枢纽是能够聚合全球高端资源的重要平台,航空运输业及航空经济可以成为带

IV. The "Silk Road in the Air" in Henan Has Improved Relations between China and Western Countries, and between China and South-South Countries

The "Silk Road in the Air" has strengthened integration between China and developed regions such as Europe, and at the same time has improved and balanced the current spatial pattern of the Belt and Road Initiative.

Located at the crossroad of Western Europe, Luxembourg has a unique geographical advantage, and can radiate to the whole European market which has about 500-million consumers, especially to surrounding EU countries such as Germany, France and Belgium. It is estimated that 40% of the EU's wealth is within a 500-kilometer radius around Luxembourg. The construction of the "Silk Road in the Air" in Henan Province has made Henan and Luxembourg important connections between China and Europe, and has promoted sustainable and in-depth economic and trade cooperation between China and the EU.

The "Silk Road in the Air" has also deepened South-South cooperation. At the end of April 2019, the project "Silk Road in the Air" South-South Partnership Alliance" was officially incorporated in the outcomes list of the Second Belt and Road Initiative International Cooperation Summit Forum. In May of the same year, the project was included in the UN Working List along with the outcomes list of the Second Summit. Taking this as an opportunity, a series of major projects such as the Global South-South Development Expo and "Silk Road in the Air" South-South Cooperation Fund are being implemented and strive to become a platform for cultural exchanges, market docking and production capacity cooperation between China and South-South countries, regions and cities, with the hope of achieving mutual market benefits and win-win cooperation.

Since its opening, the "Silk Road in the Air" has enabled Henan Province to establish close economic and trade exchanges with more than 200 countries and regions in the world, expanding the cross-border flow of goods, personnel, information, capital and services, and allowing Henan Province to participate more extensively in global industy, value and supply chains.

Henan's "Silk Road in the Air" has proved that the aviation transportation

动河南经济社会高质量发展的强大引擎。

　　在"空中丝绸之路"的助力下,河南正实现由对外开放的跟随者向内陆开放高地建设的探索者,由全球化的旁观者向国际分工体系的参与者的转变!

industry can configure high-end production elements on a global scale and promote fast-paced regional development. Henan's international aviation hub is an important platform that can drive the province's economic and social development, and aggregate global high-end resources.

With the help of the "Silk Road in the Air", Henan is realizing the transformation from a follower of opening to the outside world to an explorer of inland construction, from a globalization spectator to a participant in the international division of labor system!

第三章

寄语新未来：河南"空中丝绸之路"的趋势

Chapter 3

Outlook on the Future: Trends of the "Silk Road in the Air" in Henan Province

一、打造"一带一路"建设的河南模式

历史上的河南不仅异彩绽放,而且开放包容。作为中华民族和华夏文明的重要发祥地,在5000年中华文明史中,河南长达3000多年都是全国的政治中心、经济中心、文化中心,汇聚了东西南北的多元文化,商业文明在这里孕育发展,四大发明从这里走向世界。河南洛阳是古丝绸之路的重要节点,千百年来河南同沿线国家和地区的经贸往来绵延不断,留下了深刻的历史印记。世界上第一座人口超百万的大都市就是北宋时的汴京,即现在的河南开封,《清明上河图》中,商船云集、马帮驼队络绎不绝,生动记载了当时汴京的繁荣景象。

今天,河南紧紧抓住新一轮对外开放机遇,以"一带一路"建设为统领,加快构建内陆开放高地,推动形成全面开放新格局。不沿边、不靠海、不临江的河南,依次打通家门前的四条路,从空中、陆上、网上、海上四个维度对接"一带一路",同全球200多个国家和地区建立了贸易联系,127家世界500强企业在河南落户。

河南正以积极、主动、创新的姿态行走在"一带一路"上,推动这一伟大倡议实现高质量、惠民生、可持续的发展。"一带一路"受欢迎,不仅是因为项目本身可以带来经济红利和获得感,也来源于这一倡议背后深厚的理论与逻辑基础。

1. "一带一路"的理论魅力

道路自信的基础是理论自信,政策坚定的基础同样是理论坚定。"一带一路"的理论魅力是对"世界体系理论"的超越。世界体系理论的逻辑是"中心—边缘"秩序,而"一带一路"的逻辑是"去中心",即通过互联互通将边缘地带打通成为节点,节点之间形成网格,每一个国家都是"自中心",由此国家在网格体系中实现公平与普惠。

I. Henan's Contribution to the Belt and Road Initiative

In history, Henan not only blossomed brilliantly, but also was open and inclusive. As an important birthplace of Chinese civilization, Henan has been a political, economic and cultural center of the country for more than 3,000 years, bringing together the diverse cultures of the east, west, north and south. It is the place where commercial civilization was nurtured and developed, and from where China's Four Great Inventions were sent out into the world. Luoyang (a city in Henan Province) was an important point on the ancient Silk Road. For thousands of years, economic exchanges between Henan and countries and regions along the Silk Road were continuous, leaving a deep historical imprint. The first metropolis in the world, with a population of more than one million was Bianjing in the Northern Song Dynasty, now the city of Kaifeng in Henan Province. The Chinese painting *Riverside Scene at Qingming Festival* is a vivid record of the prosperity of Bianjing.

Today, under the guidance of the Belt and Road Initiative, Henan is seizing the opportunity of opening up and accelerating the building of an open and flourishing highland in the inland of China. Henan has opened four roads in front of its door, connecting the Belt and Road Initiative across four dimensions: air, land, sea and Internet. It has established trade links with more than 200 countries and regions in the world, and 127 of the world's top 500 enterprises have settled here.

Henan firmly adheres to the Belt and Road Initiative, advocating high-quality, sustainable and mutually beneficial development. The Belt and Road Initiative has been a success because of the deep theoretical and logical foundations of the Initiative.

1. Theoretical Charm of the Belt and Road Initiative

Confidence in the path of socialism is based on confidence in socialist theory; similarly, firm policies are based on firm theory. The theoretical charm of the Belt and Road Initiative is the transcendence of "world system theory". The logic of world system theory is "center-edge" order, while the logic of the Belt and Road Initiative is "decentralization"; that is, through connectivity, the marginal areas

世界体系理论由美国社会学家伊曼纽尔·沃勒斯坦创立,在其看来,现代世界体系是一个由经济体系、政治体系、文化体系三个基本维度构成的复合体。过去的全球化形成了以资本主义为核心的世界经济体系,"一体化"与"不平等"是这一体系的两个最主要特征。

在经济体系中,世界性劳动分工体系与世界性商品交换关系两条主线,将各个国家牢牢地粘结在庞大的世界经济网中。但是,一体化不等于均等化,相反,中心—半边缘—边缘的层级结构表明了世界经济体的极端不平等性,发达国家外围到处存在不发达。核心化以及边缘化都是动态性的过程。"中心"拥有生产和交换的双重优势,对"半边缘"和"边缘"进行经济剥削。

在政治体系中,英、美等发达国家居于体系的"中心",一些中等发达程度的国家属于体系的"半边缘",亚非拉等发展中国家处于体系的"边缘"。政治上追求霸权地位和经济上追求利润最大化一样,是资本主义世界体系的推动力。追求霸权地位是资本主义国家的共同目标。

在文化体系中,以西方文化为标准的普世价值凌驾于多元民族文化之上,营造了一种全球趋同的文化氛围。

在过去七年,"一带一路"建设有一个明显特征,就是大多数重点项目建在边缘或半边缘国家,如中亚五国、中东欧十六国、东盟十国等。这些国家很多是"内锁国"(land-locked country),如东南亚的老挝、非洲的埃塞俄比亚、中东欧的捷克等,这些国家一直被锁在大陆腹地,无法连通海洋,无法享受全球化所带来的福利。中老铁路、亚吉铁路、中欧班列等使这些"内锁国"可以连通海洋,变成"陆联国"(land-linked country),实现了陆海统筹,由此共享全球化的红利与福祉。

以中欧班列为例,其存在意义曾受质疑,被认为运量有限,纯粹是"形象工程"。从2011年首次开行到2019年4月,中欧班列累计开行了14691列,连通了中国62个城市和欧洲15个国家的51个城市,铺行的路线达到68条。从总量上看,中欧班列的确远远没有达到海运的规模,

are opened up as nodes, and a grid is formed based on the nodes. Every country is "self-centered", so that the country can realize fairness and universal benefits in the grid system.

The theory of the world system was founded by Emanuel Wallerstein, an American sociologist in New York. In his opinion, the modern world system is a complex composed of three basic dimensions: the economic system, political system and cultural system. In the past, globalization formed a world economic system with capitalism as the core. "Integration" and "inequality" are the two most important features of this system.

In the economic system, the world division of labor system and the world commodity exchange relationship are the two main lines, which firmly bind every country in a world economic network. However, integration is not equalization. On the contrary, the "center—semi-edge—edge" hierarchy indicates the extreme inequality of the world economy: underdevelopment is everywhere on the periphery of developed countries. Both centralization and marginalization are dynamic processes. The "center" has the dual advantages of production and exchange, economically exploiting the "semi-edge" and "edge" countries.

In the political system, developed countries such as the United Kingdom and the United States are at the "center" of the system, some moderately developed countries are at the "semi-edge" of the system, and developing countries such as Asia, Africa, Latin America are at the "edge" of the system. The political pursuit of hegemony and the economic pursuit of profit maximization are the driving forces of the capitalist world system. The pursuit of hegemonic status is the common goal of capitalist countries.

In the cultural system, the universal values of Western culture are superior to the multinational culture, creating a cultural atmosphere of global convergence.

In the past seven years, the Belt and Road Initiative has been characterized by the fact that most of its key projects have been built in "edge" or "semi-edge" countries, such as the five central Asian countries, 16 central and eastern European countries, and 10 ASEAN countries. Many of these countries are land-locked countries, such as Laos, Ethiopia, and the Czech Republic. They have been locked in the hinterland of their respective continents, unable to connect to the sea or enjoy the benefits brought by globalization. The China-Laos Railway, Addis

第三章 寄语新未来：河南"空中丝绸之路"的趋势

按照编组规定，每一列编组41车，每车装两个标准集装箱计算，2017年中欧班列总共运输30万标箱，8年累计82万标箱，而全球海运2017年运输就达2.38亿标箱，中欧班列甚至低于一个长江内河码头的运输量。但是，从国际关系层面、从全球公共产品层面来看，中欧班列对地缘政治影响很大。这种影响不是大国博弈，而是使途经的国家能够同时面向大西洋和太平洋，实现了真正的开放与全球化。

在新冠肺炎疫情背景下，中欧班列的常态化稳定运行有助于降低疫情对中欧产业链、供应链合作带来的冲击和影响，发挥国际运输新动

Ababa-Djibouti Railway and the China-Europe freight railway have enabled these "land-locked countries" to connect with the sea and become "land-linked countries", thus able to share the benefits of globalization.

Let's take the China-Europe freight railway as an example. It was once regarded as a "prestige project" with limited traffic volume. Between its opening in 2011 and April 2019, a total of 14,691 China-Europe freight trains were launched, connecting 62 cities in China and 51 cities in 15 European countries, with 68 routes in operation. From the perspective of total amount, China-Europe freight trains cannot reach the scale of shipping. According to the regulations, each freight train has 41 cars, and each car carries two standard containers. In 2017 global marine transport reached 238 million TEU; while China-Europe freight trains transport reached only 300,000 TEU, accumulating a total of 820,000 TEU in 8 years. The freight volume of China-Europe freight trains was even lower than that of a Yangtze River port. However, from the perspectives of international relations and global public good, China-Europe freight trains have a great impact on geopolitics. This impact is not the game of great powers, but enables the countries along the Road to communicate with the Atlantic and Pacific Oceans, realizing true openness and globalization.

In the context of the COVID-19 epidemic, the regular and stable operation of the China-Europe freight trains will help reduce the impact of the epidemic on the China-Europe industrial and supply chain cooperation, and play the role of a new artery of international transport. Compared with air transport and sea transport, international railway transport has the advantages of less quarantine restrictions and relatively safe and stable operation. In the first quarter of 2020, a total of 1,941 China-Europe freight trains were launched, delivering 174,000 standard containers of goods, an increase of 15% and 18% respectively over the same period of last year. By the end of April 2020, 448,000 medical supply items, a total of 1,440 tons, had been delivered by China-Europe freight trains to Italy, Germany, Spain, the Czech Republic, Poland, Hungary, the Netherlands, Lithuania and other countries, and from those countries epidemic prevention supplies had been allocated to more European countries. The China-Europe freight trains, which run across the Eurasian Continent, not only bring much-needed epidemic prevention supplies to Europe, but also regards and care from

脉的作用。相比空运和海运，国际铁路联运分段运输具有人员检疫限制相对较少、运行相对安全稳定的优势。2020年一季度，中欧班列共开行1941列，发运货物17.4万标箱，同比分别增长15%和18%。截至2020年4月底，中欧班列已累计发运防疫物资44.8万件，共计1440吨，送达意大利、德国、西班牙、捷克、波兰、匈牙利、荷兰、立陶宛等多国，并以这些国家为节点分拨到更多的欧洲国家。中欧班列横穿亚欧大陆，给欧洲载去的不仅是急需的抗疫物资，更是来自东方的温暖与关爱，为中欧携手抗疫增添信心与力量。

总之，"一带一路"不能只是政策分析或政策解读，要有"原理论"；不能总是讲"一带一路"不是什么，而是要讲清楚"一带一路"是什么，即她的具体内涵以及衡量指标究竟是什么。"一带一路"的逻辑有三个层次：第一，中国经济外交的顶层设计；第二，践行人类命运共同体的重要实践；第三，中国参与全球治理的公共产品。

当今世界各国面临百年未有之大变局，经济面临严峻的下行压力，经济全球化遭遇波折，多边主义受到冲击，国际金融市场震荡，国际大宗商品价格大幅波动，不稳定、不确定因素明显增加。对中国而言，外部输入性风险上升。在此背景下，改革开放依然取得新突破，共建"一带一路"取得重要进展。

"一带一路"建设更具层次性、系统性。自由贸易港、粤港澳大湾区、国际进口博览会等重大事业的落地与推动，使"一带一路"有了更具体、更强有力的支撑体系，实现了陆海联动、内外联动、政企联动。共建"一带一路"引领效应持续释放，同沿线国家的合作机制不断健全，经贸合作和人文交流加快推进。截至2019年4月，已有125个国家和29个国际组织同中国签署173份"一带一路"合作文件，古老的"丝绸之路"越来越以崭新的姿态焕发生机。由于合作国家数量的增多，所以今天中国提出"丝路共建国家"，取代过去"64+1"模式以及后来的"丝路沿线国家+丝路相关国家"模式。就"一带一路"贸易畅通而

China. This adds confidence and strength to our joint fight against the epidemic.

In short, the comprehensive understanding of the Belt and Road Initiative should not only be about policy analysis or policy interpretation, but also theory. It's essential to figure out what the Belt and Road Initiative is, namely what its specific connotation is and what the measurement index is. The logic of the Belt and Road Initiative has three levels: (1) the top-level design of China's economic diplomacy; (2) the important practice of building a community with a shared future for mankind; (3) the public goods of global governance in which China participates.

Countries today are facing major changes unseen in a century. Their economies are under severe downward pressure. Economic globalization is facing twists and turns, multilateralism is under threat, the international financial market is in turmoil, international commodity prices are fluctuating sharply, and instability and uncertainty are clearly on the rise. For China, imported risks are rising. Against this backdrop, new breakthroughs have been made in the process of Reform and Opening Up, and significant progress has been made in jointly building the Belt and Road Initiative.

The Belt and Road Initiative is hierarchical and systematic. The launch and promotion of such major undertakings as the Free Trade Port, the Guangdong-Hong Kong-Macao Greater Bay Area and the International Import Expo have provided a concrete and powerful support system for the Belt and Road Initiative, and enabled the government to interact with enterprises on land and sea, both inside and outside China. Cooperation mechanisms with countries along the Belt and Road have been improved and economic and trade cooperation as well as cultural exchanges have been accelerated. By April 2019, 125 countries and 29 international organizations had signed 173 the Belt and Road Initiative cooperation documents with China, and the ancient Silk Road was gaining new vitality. Due to the increase in the number of cooperative countries, China puts forward the idea of "Silk Road Partner Countries" to replace the "64 + 1" model of the past and the later "Countries along and Related to the Silk Road" model. As far as Belt and Road Initiative trade flows are concerned, the first thing that comes to mind is the success of overseas economic and trade cooperation zones, 113 of which have been established around the world. In the past few years,

言，大家首先想到的是境外经济贸易合作区，目前已经在全球建立了113个。过去几年，跨境电商综合实验区纷纷成立，这有助于"数字丝绸之路"建设。陆、海、空、冰、网等"一带一路"建设领域不断拓展。

"一带一路"强调"双向属性"，既要看"走出去"项目，也要关注"引进来"效果。中国大幅压缩外资准入负面清单，扩大金融、汽车等行业开放，一批重大外资项目落地，新设外资企业大幅增长。未来将进一步加大吸引外资力度。进一步放宽市场准入，缩减外资准入负面清单，允许更多领域实行外资独资经营。促进贸易和投资自由化便利化始

comprehensive pilot zones for cross-border e-commerce have been set up to help build a "Digital Silk Road". The Belt and Road Initiative construction fields, such as land, sea, air, ice and Internet, have been continuously expanded.

The Belt and Road Initiative emphasizes the "two-way property", which not only pays attention to the "outbound" project, but also attaches importance to the effect of "bringing in". China opened many industries to the outside world, including the financial sector and the auto industry. A number of major foreign-funded projects were launched, and new foreign-investment enterprises grew rapidly. In the future, China will devote greater efforts to attracting foreign investment, further relax restrictions on market access, reduce the blacklist for foreign investment, and allow more areas to operate with sole foreign investment. Promoting free trade and facilitating investment have always been China's standpoint in fully integrating itself with the world. China firmly upholds economic globalization and free trade, and actively participates in the reform of the WTO. We will accelerate the building of a network of high-standard free trade zones and continue to promote China-U.S. economic consultations. China will not pursue an exclusive trade policy; instead, we will foster a fair and free market environment in which domestic and foreign enterprises are treated as equals and can enjoy fair competition.

In the new pattern of opening up, flowing opening up is transforming to institutional opening up. We will open up to the outside world in a more rule-based and institutional way. Institutional opening up emphasizes the "soft connectivity" of rules, standards, qualifications and intellectual property rights, which is the traditional advantage of Western developed countries. Over the past 500 years, Western developed countries have built their institutional voice through the ocean, and through finance, rules, standards and values. At the initial stage of opening up, "edge" or "semi-edge" countries can only choose flowing opening up, relying on commodities, factors, energy resources and labor costs, and such opening up remains at a low level and lacks initiative. Institutional opening up is about a smart economy and a brand economy, driven by innovation and talents. Of course, the foundation of institutional opening up is to master the "key technologies, key parts and components, and key raw materials", demonstrate advanced societal progress at the cultural and value levels, and acquire

终是中国充分与世界"互融"的立场、原则与价值观。中国坚定维护经济全球化和自由贸易,积极参与世贸组织改革。加快构建高标准自贸区网络,继续推动中美经贸磋商。中国不会在贸易层面推行排他性政策,而是要营造内、外资企业一视同仁、公平竞争的公正市场环境,要营造自由贸易的国际市场环境。

从流动性开放到制度性开放。全面开放新格局,新在以"一带一路"为重点,从推动商品和要素流动性开放,到更加注重规则等制度性开放。制度性开放强调规则、标准、资质、知识产权等"软联通",这是西方发达国家的传统优势。过去500年,西方发达国家通过海洋,通过金融、规则、标准、价值观等建立了制度性话语权。边缘或半边缘国家在开放初期只能选择流动性开放,靠商品、靠要素、靠能源资源、靠劳动力成本优势,但是汗水经济、通道经济、飞地经济总体还是低水平开放,主动性不强。制度性开放是智慧经济、品牌经济,是创新驱动、人才驱动。当然制度性开放的基础要掌握"关键工艺、关键零部件、关键原材料",在文化和价值层面要展现推动人类社会进步的先进性,同时要通过多边主义、制度主义合作获得国际塑造能力。"一带一路"是一种公共产品,已经从物质性、理念性属性,向制度性属性拓展。

"一带一路"建设是具体的、实践的,在微观层面,要靠企业,不仅靠中国企业,也要推动国际优秀企业的参与,加强第三方市场合作。"一带一路"建设需要法治化、便利化的营商环境,需要具有企业家精神的企业。2019年10月,在世界银行最新发布的《2020年营商环境报告》中,中国排名再次大幅上升15位,排名第31位。这是继上年由第78名提升至第46名之后又一重大进步。

international influence through multilateralism and institutional cooperation. The Belt and Road Initiative is a kind of public goods, which has expanded from being material to institutional.

The construction of the Belt and Road Initiative is concrete and practical. At the micro level, it should rely on enterprises, not only Chinese enterprises, but also outstanding international enterprises to strengthen cooperation in the third market. It requires a law-based and business-friendly environment. In the World Bank's latest *2020 Doing Business Report* released in October 2019, China jumped another 15 places to the 31st. It was another significant improvement after the previous year's rise from the 78th to the 46th place.

> **Column: The Brilliant Opening-Up of Henan**
>
> On August 26, 2019, the State Council Information Office held a series of provincial (regional and municipal) press conferences. Wang Guosheng, then Secretary of the CPC Henan Provincial Committee and Director of the then Standing Committee of Henan Provincial People's Congress, and Chen Run'er, then Deputy Secretary of the CPC Henan Provincial Committee and Governor of People's Government of Henan Province introduced the theme of "the brilliant opening-up Henan Province" and answered questions from reporters.
>
> Wang Guosheng introduced opening-up Henan:
>
> ► We will continue to develop both advanced manufacturing and modern service industries, and develop strategic emerging industries while upgrading traditional industries. We will strive to attract large and strong industries and undertake industrial relocation, and make equipment manufacturing and food manufacturing toward a trillion level.
>
> ►Smart phones, new energy passenger cars, shield tunneling machines, and opto-electronic chips made in Henan Province will become our new business card. UU Errand will become the largest shared errand platform in China, and the logistics industry will become the first in China.
>
> ► The first biological breeding industrial innovation center in China was established in Henan, and Shenzhou spacecraft, high-speed railway

专栏:开放的河南更出彩

2019年8月26日,国务院新闻办公室举行省(区、市)系列新闻发布会,时任中共河南省委书记、河南省人大常委会主任王国生,时任中共河南省委副书记、河南省人民政府省长陈润儿围绕"开放的河南更出彩"作介绍,并答记者问。

王国生介绍开放的河南:

▶打好产业结构优化升级牌,坚持发展先进制造业和壮大现代服务业并举,培育战略性新兴产业和改造提升传统产业并行,着力招大引强、承接产业转移,装备制造、食品制造跃向万亿级产业。

▶智能手机、新能源客车、盾构机、光电子芯片等成为河南制造新名片,UU跑腿成为全国最大的共享跑腿平台,物流业迈入全国第一方阵。

▶全国首个生物育种产业创新中心落户河南,神舟飞船、高铁等大国重器上有了更多河南元素。

▶打好基础能力建设牌,郑州机场二期建成投运、三期工程启动建设,率先实现米字形高铁网实质性落地,全国重要的综合交通枢纽、通信枢纽、能源基地地位不断巩固。

▶卢森堡货航加密至每周18班,郑州机场客货运吞吐量跃居中部地区首位。中欧班列(郑州)每周14去10回,成为欧亚大陆桥的一支活跃"驼队"。

▶全球跨境电子商务大会永久落户郑州,首创"1210"监管服务模式,河南E贸易辐射190多个国家和地区,成为全球网购商品集疏分拨中心。

▶129家世界500强企业在这里落户,郑煤机、浙减、大森机电等河南企业成功开展跨国并购。

and other heavy equipment of our country have been witnessing Henan's contribution.

➤ The second phase of Zhengzhou Airport construction was already put into operation and the third phase of this project has been started up. The implementation of the high-speed rail lines extending in eight directions has been established, consolidating the position of Henan as an important comprehensive transportation and communications hub in China.

➤ Cargolux Airlines International increased its flights to 18 per week. Zhengzhou Airport ranked first in the central region in passenger and cargo throughput. Every week, 14 China-Europe freight trains (Zhengzhou) go to Europe and 10 return to Zhengzhou, becoming an active "camel team" on the Eurasia Land Bridge.

➤ The Global Cross-border E-commerce Conference will be permanently settled in Zhengzhou, initiating the "1210" supervision and service model. Henan's e-trade has reached more than 190 countries and regions, making it a collection and distribution center of global online shopping goods.

➤ 129 Fortune Global 500 Companies have settled here; Henan enterprises such as Zhengzhou Coal Mining Machinery Group Co., Ltd., Xijian Automobile Shock Absorber Co., Ltd. and Henan Dasen Mechanical and Electrical Co., Ltd. successfully carried out cross-border mergers and acquisitions.

➤ The agricultural products processing industry has become the first pillar industry of Henan, with nearly 8,000 big enterprises. More and more agricultural enterprises are going global and taking root in countries and regions along the Belt and Road.

➤ By the end of June 2019, the number of market entities in the province had exceeded 6 million, ranking fifth in China and first in central China.

In the future, the Henan Government will continue to optimize the political environment, the legal environment and the living environment,

▶农产品加工业已经成为河南工业的第一大支柱产业，规模以上企业近8000家，越来越多的农业企业正在走出去，在"一带一路"沿线国家和地区"生根发芽"。

▶截至2019年6月底，全省市场主体突破了600万户，这个数量在全国是第五位、在中部地区是首位。

未来，河南将继续优化政务环境、法治环境、生活环境，在权力上做减法、服务上做加法，努力让审批事项最少、办理速度最快、规则最公平、程序最规范，让一流的营商环境成为河南的新标识。

2. "一带一路"高质量发展需要企业家精神

2017年9月25日，中共中央国务院下发了《中共中央国务院关于营造企业家健康成长环境弘扬优秀企业家精神更好发挥企业家作用的意见》。这一文件被称为"史无前例"的文件，是首次以中央专门文件的形式，明确了企业家精神的重要地位和价值。企业家精神的关键内涵是两个词：文脉、商脉，两者相互助益、缺一不可，这两个词汇也是"一带一路"高质量发展的关键词。

五年的企业靠产品、十年的企业靠技术、百年的企业靠文化。对企业家而言，文脉就是要在企业内部塑造归属和依赖，在外部建立欣赏与认同，要激发国际社会分享中国企业的冲动。

在"一带一路"建设中，政府是主导，企业是主体。中国企业不仅要走出去，更要走进去、走上去，不仅要实现产业化，更要实现品牌化、国际化。

回顾中国企业进入世界500强的历程，我们可以发现，1954年，美国《财富》杂志开始对全球企业做排行，直到1989年才出现了第一家中国内地企业——中国银行。1995年，中国内地企业当时只有三家企业

and will decrease the power but improve the service of governmental agencies. We will make every effort to minimize the number of examination and approval items, make the transaction of business fastest, formulate the fairest rules and the most standardized procedures, so that the first-class business environment will become a new symbol of Henan.

2. High-quality Development of the Belt and Road Initiative Requires Entrepreneurship

On September 25, 2017, the State Council of the CPC Central Committee issued *Opinions of the State Council of the CPC Central Committee on Creating a Healthy Environment for Entrepreneurs to Grow Up, Carrying Forward the Excellent Entrepreneurial Spirit and Better Playing the Role of Entrepreneurs*. This, considered as "unprecedented", is the first official document formulated by the Central Leadership to define the importance and value of entrepreneurship. The key connotations of entrepreneurship are cultural spirit and business spirit, which are mutually beneficial and indispensable. These two phrases are also key words for the high-quality development of the Belt and Road Initiative.

A five-year enterprise relies on products, a ten-year enterprise relies on technology, and a century-old enterprise relies on culture. For entrepreneurs, cultural spirit means building a sense of ownership and dependence inside the enterprise, building appreciation and identity outside, and stimulating the international community's impulse to share Chinese enterprises.

In the Belt and Road Initiative, the government plays the leading role and enterprises are the main players. Chinese enterprises should not only realize industrialization, but also branding and internationalization.

Looking back at the history of Chinese enterprises entering the world's top 500 companies, we can find that it was not until 1989 that the first mainland Chinese enterprise—Bank of China—ranked on a list of global companies according to U.S. *Fortune* magazine. In 1995, there were only three mainland Chinese companies on the list: Bank of China, Sinochem and COFCO, compared to 149 Japanese enterprises, 151 American enterprises and 300 in the United States and Japan combined in the same year. However, Chinese enterprises are developing

上榜——中国银行、中化集团、中粮集团。而日本企业在1995年达到149家，美国151家，美日两国加起来300家。但是，中国企业发展速度很快，到2015年的时候有106家企业进入世界500强，首次破百。之后，2016年是110家，2017年115家，2018年是120家，2019年达到129家，首次超过美国企业。但是入榜的企业中，国有企业很多，民营企业太少。而且，很多企业昙花一现，入榜不易，但掉榜很快，如安邦保险、华信能源等。所以，"一带一路"就是要倒逼中国企业改革，要有飞洋过海的艺术，关键是要有企业家精神。

打造河南模式的关键是要努力成为孵化中国企业家精神的摇篮。建议成立丝路企业家商学院，商学院的定位不仅要助益河南企业，更要助力于参加"一带一路"的所有中国企业。中国现在缺的不是企业，缺的是有品牌价值、充分国际化的优秀企业。"一带一路"缺的不是产品，缺的是能够赢得尊重的精品。

> **专栏：河南企业积极开拓"一带一路"沿线市场**
>
> 凭借良好的品牌形象，河南知名企业宇通客车的海外市场不断扩大，出口量节节攀升，单笔订单的数量和金额屡创新高。2019年，宇通出口英国第500辆客车成功交付，168辆高品质客车交付乌兹别克斯坦，批量机场摆渡车交付西班牙与摩洛哥，20辆纯电动客车驶入丹麦，33辆纯电动客车交付芬兰，10辆纯电动城间车出口法国，63辆双源无轨电车陆续驶入墨西哥等。
>
> 此外，作为中国最早、最大也是综合实力最强的拖拉机制造企业，中国一拖集团早在2008年就在全球100多个国家建立了营销网络，完成了销售的全球布局。近年来，为加快国际化步伐、努力成为全球卓越的农业装备供应商，在"一带一路"倡议的引领下，中国一拖积极开拓"一带一路"沿线国家和地区市场，承

rapidly. By 2015, 106 enterprises had entered the world top 500. By 2016 the list included 110 Chinese enterprises, 115 by 2017, 120 by 2018, and 129 by 2019, surpassing American companies for the first time. Among the companies on the list, there are many state-owned enterprises but few private ones. What's more, many enterprises, such as Anbang Insurance Group and CEFC China Energy Company Limited are ephemeral, soon disappearing from the list. Therefore, the Belt and Road Initiative is to force Chinese enterprises to reform. Chinese enterprises must be equipped with arts which can spread abroad and entrepreneurship in especial.

The key to building the Henan model is to strive to become the cradle of China's entrepreneurial spirit. The next step is to establish a silk road business school for entrepreneurs. The positioning of the business school should not only help Henan enterprises, but also help all Chinese enterprises participating in the Belt and Road Initiative. What China lacks is not enterprises, but exceptional enterprises with brand value and full internationalization. What the Belt and Road Initiative lacks is not products, but a quality product that can win respect.

Column: Henan Enterprises Actively Expand Markets along the Belt and Road Initiative Route

With a good brand image, Zhengzhou Yutong Bus Co., Ltd., a well-known enterprise in Henan Province, has been expanding its overseas markets and increasing its export volume. The amount and the sum of a single order have reached new highs. By 2019, Yutong had exported 500 passenger cars to UK, 168 high quality passenger trains to Uzbekistan, a great number of airport shuttle buses to Spain and Morocco, 20 electric buses to Denmark, 33 electric passenger cars to Finland, 10 electric intercity cars to France and 63 dual-source trolleybuses to Mexico.

In addition, as the earliest and largest tractor manufacturing enterprise with the strongest comprehensive strength in China, YTO Group Corporation had established a global marketing network in more than 100 countries by 2008. In recent years, YTO Group Corporation has made every effort to speed up its pace of internationalization, aiming to become

> 载着中国农机光荣与梦想的"东方红"品牌在"一带一路"沿线国家和地区闪耀。2011年,中国一拖集团曾收购法国农机公司McCormick,实现了新中国成立后中国农机企业收购世界级农机企业零的突破。在白俄罗斯,一拖将与白俄罗斯明斯克拖拉机厂在中白园区内合作建立研发中心和生产基地,"抢滩"东欧和中亚农机市场,这也是"洛阳制造"首次借力"一带一路"旗舰项目出海。

3. 河南未来在"一带一路"建设中发挥更大作用的几点建议

(1)增强"空中丝绸之路"的示范、带动作用。

2017年6月14日,国家主席习近平在会见卢森堡首相贝泰尔时强调,中方支持建设郑州—卢森堡"空中丝绸之路"。与国内其他省份对接东南亚、中亚等发展中国家不同,河南对接的是西欧发达国家。因此要超越"通道经济"模式,在智慧经济、品牌经济上做文章,要努力打造中欧"一带一路"合作的优秀样板。要重视产能合作,大力发展高端制造业、新基建、跨境电子商务等新兴业态,不断充实健康丝绸之路与数字丝绸之路。积极推进金融合作,提供更多优质的金融产品,为海外企业"引进来"和内陆地区企业"走出去"提供新动力。

(2)增强河南智慧对接"一带一路"的能力。

"一带一路"需要高端的专业服务业,如熟悉国际业务的会计审计、评级机构、战略咨询机构等。著名的评级公司,如穆迪、惠誉、标普等,总部都在美国。国际社会最著名的战略咨询公司,如ADL、麦肯锡、波士顿、贝恩咨询,总部也全都在美国。四大会计师事务所,三个总部在英国伦敦,一个总部在荷兰首都阿姆斯特丹。这些公司是轻资产,但非常关键,对美欧企业国际化进行"把脉",避免了重复试错,降低了国际化风险。中国企业也需要这类能够实现智慧对接的专业服务,这是痛点,也是机遇。

the world's most outstanding agricultural equipment supplier. Under the lead of the Belt and Road Initiative, YTO Group Corporation is actively expanding markets in the countries and regions along the Belt and Road Initiative route. The brand "Oriental Red" carries forth China's agricultural machinery spirit and ambition. In 2011, YTO Group Corporation acquired McCormick, a French agricultural machinery company. This was the first acquisition of world-class agricultural machinery enterprise by a Chinese agricultural machinery enterprise since the establishment of the People's Republic of China. YTO Group Corporation will cooperate with Minsk Tractor Factory in Republic of Belarus to establish a research and development center and production base in the China-Belarus Industrial Park, then open the agricultural machinery market of Eastern Europe and Central Asia. This is also the first time that "Made in Luoyang" has taken advantage of the Belt and Road Initiative to go abroad.

3. Suggestions for Henan to Play a Bigger Role in the Construction of the Belt and Road Initiative in the Future

First, the leading role of the "Silk Road in the Air" should be enhanced.

On June 14, 2017, when meeting with Luxembourg Prime Minister Xavier Bettel, Chinese President Xi Jinping stressed that China supports the construction of the Zhengzhou-Luxembourg "Silk Road in the Air". Unlike other provinces in China, which are connected to developing countries such as Southeast Asia and Central Asia, Henan is connected to developed countries in Western Europe. Therefore, it is necessary to go beyond the "channel economy" model and create a model for China-Europe Belt and Road Initiative cooperation in terms of smart economy and brand economy. We should attach importance to production capacity cooperation, vigorously develop high-end manufacturing, new infrastructure, cross-border E-commerce and other emerging businesses, and build a healthy Silk Road and digital Silk Road. We will continuously promote financial cooperation and provide more high-quality financial products to attract overseas enterprises and enable inland enterprises to "go global".

Second, the capacity of Henan's professional services and agencies to serve the Belt and Road Initiative needs to be increased.

（3）加强"一带一路"的专业化智库建设。

"一带一路"倡议提出后，很多高校、企业、地方都成立了专门研究机构，但"多而不强、有库无智"的问题依然突显。目前，国内智库大多在论证"一带一路"的重要性，缺乏具体咨询建议和长期跟踪研究的长效机制。建议在郑州成立"一带一路"研究院，这一研究院应兼具研究、倡议、行动能力：一是与政府职能部门和一线中国企业做好深度对接，提供管用与接地气的智库产品；二是要探索区域和国别问题研究的新路径，善用大数据等新研究工具，及时监测"一带一路"民意变化，尤其是社交网络上涉及"一带一路"的民意热点；三是注重强化

The Belt and Road Initiative requires high-end professional services, such as accounting and auditing agencies, along with rating and strategic consulting agencies that are familiar with international business. Famous rating companies, such as Moody, Fitch Ratings, Standard and Poor's Credit Rating, are headquartered in the United States. The most famous strategic consulting firms in the international community, such as ADL, McKinsey, Boston, and Bain, are all headquartered in the United States, too. Three of the big four accounting firms are based in London and one in Amsterdam, the capital of the Netherlands. Asset-light as they are, these companies are crucial in allowing American and European companies to avoid errors and risks associated with internationalization. Chinese enterprises also need these kinds of professional services. This is our shortcoming but also an opportunity.

Third, the construction of specialized Belt and Road Initiative think tanks requires further strengthening.

After the Belt and Road Initiative was put forward, many universities, enterprises and local governments set up specialized research institutions. At present, most domestic think tanks lack mechanisms for long-term consultation and follow-up research. A necessary step is to establish a Belt and Road research institute in Zhengzhou. This institute should have the ability to conduct research, give advice and take action. Firstly, it should be deeply connected with government functional departments and first-line Chinese enterprises, so as to provide effective and down-to-earth results. Secondly, it should explore new ways to study regional and national issues, make use of new research tools such as big data, and monitor the change of public opinion on the Belt and Road Initiative, especially the public opinion hot spots on social networks. Thirdly, it should focus on strengthening "strategic communication" and effectively and accurately promoting the Belt and Road Initiative in the international community.

Fourth, cooperation in third-party markets is in demand.

Third-party market cooperation refers to partnerships between two countries in developing markets in a third country. This mode of international cooperation, upholding the spirit of "mutual consultation, joint development and benefits sharing" of the Belt and Road Initiative, will integrate China's production capacity, the advanced technology of developed countries and the development needs of

"战略传播",有效精准地在国际社会讲好"一带一路"故事。

（4）加强第三方市场合作。

第三方市场合作指两国合作开发第三方国家市场,是一种国际合作新模式,秉持"一带一路"建设"共商、共建、共享"的精神,这种国际合作新模式将中国的优势产能、发达国家的先进技术和广大发展中国家的发展需求有效对接,共同为第三国经济发展注入新动能。2018年5月,在国务院总理李克强和日本首相安倍晋三的共同见证下,两国签署了《关于中日企业开展第三方市场合作的备忘录》,同意在中日经济高层对话框架下建立推进中日第三方市场合作工作机制。目前,包括英国、荷兰、德国、瑞士等国家都有强烈的意向深度参与第三方市场合作,这种合作方式不仅为中国与西方发达国家共建"一带一路"开辟了新空间,也有利于中国的产业链升级。

总之,"一带一路"越来越成为新型全球化进程中的一抹亮色,这一倡议将助益中国经济从高速度增长转变为高质量发展,将助益中国企业完成国际化布局,将助益郑州等中国城市实现跨越式发展,将助益国际社会实现公平、包容、普惠发展。

developing countries, to facilitate economic development in the third country. In May 2018, Chinese Premier of the State Council Li Keqiang and Japanese Prime Minister Shinzo Abe witnessed the signing of the *Memorandum on Cooperation in Third-party Markets between Chinese and Japanese Enterprises*, agreeing to establish cooperation in third-party markets and undertake high-level economic dialogue between China and Japan. At present, many countries, including the UK, Netherlands, Germany and Switzerland, have strong intention to participate in third-party market cooperation. This mode of cooperation not only opens up new space for China and developed countries to jointly build the Belt and Road Initiative, but also helps to upgrade China's industrial chain.

The Belt and Road Initiative is becoming a bright spot in the new globalization process, and assisting China's economic transition from high speed growth to high quality development. The initiative will help Chinese enterprises achieve internationalization, will help Zhengzhou and other Chinese cities achieve rapid development, and will promote fair, inclusive and common development in the international community.

二、最佳"一带一路"国际航空物流业合作实践[1]

2014年初,河南航投完成对卢森堡货航35%股权的收购,由此开启中—卢两国航空物流业的紧密合作。

7年过去,双方的合作果实丰硕:卢森堡货航在郑州机场的航班量由每周2班加密至18班,通航点由3个增加至16个城市,航线覆盖欧美亚三大洲的24个国家100多个城市;累计为郑州机场贡献国际货运量近60万吨,对郑州机场货运增长量贡献为79%,成为郑州机场货运的增长龙头;带动卢森堡货航的国际排名由合作初期的第九位提升到第六位。

---

[1]本章节作者为卢森堡国际货运航空公司董事长保罗·海明格。

II. International Aviation Logistics Cooperation under the Belt and Road Initiative [1]

In early 2014, Henan Civil Aviation Development and Investment Co., Ltd. acquired a 35% stake in Cargolux Airlines International, thus initiating close cooperation in the aviation logistics industry between China and Luxembourg.

In the past seven years, the cooperation between the two parties has been fruitful: The number of flights of Cargolux Airlines International at Zhengzhou Airport has increased from 2 to 18 per week, the number of destinations has increased from 3 cities to 16, and the flight routes cover more than 100 cities in 24 countries in Europe, America and Asia. The cooperative project has contributed nearly 600,000 tons of international cargo to Zhengzhou Airport, a massive 79% increase. The international ranking of Cargolux Airlines International was improved from the ninth place in the early stage of cooperation to the sixth.

1. Win-win Cooperation and Steady Progress

The 2008 global financial crisis brought a long-term negative impact on economic growth in the Eurozone. In 2013, the European aviation logistics industry suffered from three pressures: the continuous downturn of the Eurozone economy, the rising oil price, and the uncertainty and instability of the world economy, all of which suppressed the development of international trade. The development of the aviation logistics market is sensitive to macroeconomic fluctuations. Under such circumstances, Cargolux Airlines International carried out equity restructuring through international bidding, and Henan Civil Aviation Development and Investment Co., Ltd. became the second shareholder of Cargolux Airlines International, and the first non-EU overseas investor.

After equity restructuring, with the support of the Henan Provincial Government and Henan Civil Aviation Development and Investment Co., Ltd., the Zhengzhou-Luxembourg route of Henan's "Silk Road in the Air" was opened

---

[1] The author of this chapter is Paul Helminger, Chairman of Cargolux Airlines International.

1. 双赢合作，行稳致远

2008年全球金融危机为欧元区经济增长带来长期的负面影响。2013年，欧洲航空物流业遭遇了三重压力：欧元区经济持续下行、石油价格不断升高、世界经济的不确定性和不稳定性直接打压国际贸易的发展。航空物流市场的发展对宏观经济波动较为敏感，卢森堡货航在上述背景下通过国际招标方式进行了股权重组，河南航投成为卢森堡货航的第二大股东，也是第一个非欧盟的海外投资方。

股权重组后，在河南省政府及河南航投大力支持下，河南"空中丝绸之路"郑州—卢森堡航线于2014年6月开通，至当年11月，在短短5个月内货运量突破了10 000吨，该运量占郑州新郑国际机场同期货运增量的23.4%，占机场同期国际货运增量的29.3%。新股东的进入、新市场的开发，让卢森堡货航在重组完成的当年，就获得业务量的强劲增长，并为股东带来经济回报，卢森堡货航与河南航投之间的合作信心和动力逐步增加。

2015年9月，作为一家国际化企业，卢森堡货航首次在郑州召开董事会。随后，董事会成员和企业高管又访问了河南多地，进一步了解郑州、了解河南、了解中国这个巨大的新兴市场。

卢森堡货航与河南航投的良好合作在取得良好经济效益的同时，也发挥了更大的社会效益，并促进、加深了卢—中两国之间的密切合作。

2017年6月，卢森堡首相贝泰尔来华进行国事访问，中国国家主席习近平在会见时指出，要深化双方在"一带一路"建设框架内金融和产能等合作，中方支持建设郑州—卢森堡"空中丝绸之路"。

2018年4月，卢森堡旅游签证（郑州）便捷服务平台落成，在郑州可以直接办理卢森堡签证。由于河南赴欧旅游人数逐年递增，赴欧签证业务需求量不断增加，在卢森堡驻华大使馆管辖区办理的签证业务中，河南仅次于北京，排名第二。

2019年3月末，在亚洲博鳌2019年年会上，卢森堡同中国签署了

in June 2014, and in November of that year, the freight volume surpassed 10,000 tons in a span of 5 months, which accounted for 23.4% of Zhengzhou Xinzheng International Airport's freight increment and 29.3% of the airport's international freight increment over the corresponding period. The entry of new shareholders and the development of new markets enabled Cargolux Airlines International to achieve strong growth in business volume and brought economic returns to shareholders in the same year after the equity restructuring. Cooperation between Henan Civil Aviation Development and Investment Co., Ltd. and Cargolux Airlines International has been steadily increasing.

In September 2015, Cargolux Airlines International held its first board meeting in Zhengzhou. Later, board members and executives visited many locations in Henan Province to learn more about Zhengzhou, Henan and China, a huge emerging market.

The cooperation between Cargolux Airlines International and Henan Civil Aviation Development and Investment Co., Ltd. not only produces economic benefits, but also produces social benefits, as well as deepening the relationship between the two countries.

In June 2017, Prime Minister of Luxembourg Xavier Bettel paid a state visit to China. During the meeting, Chinese President Xi Jinping pointed out the need to deepen China-Luxembourg cooperation in finance and production capacity within the framework of the Belt and Road Initiative, and expressed that China supports the building of the Zhengzhou-Luxembourg "Silk Road in the Air".

In April 2018, the Luxembourg Tourist Visa Convenient Service Platform was launched in Zhengzhou, where clients can directly apply for a Luxembourg visa. The number of tourists from Henan Province to Europe increases, and so does the demand for European visas. Among the visa applications handled by the Luxembourg embassy in China, Henan Province ranks second only to Beijing.

At the Boao Asia Annual Conference at the end of March, 2019, Luxembourg signed the Belt and Road Initiative cooperation document with China, becoming the second EU founding member after Italy to join the Belt and Road Initiative.

Since the construction of the "Silk Road in the Air" between Henan and Luxembourg, cooperation between the two countries has been continuously strengthened. The Belt and Road Initiative Economic Cooperation Forum has

"一带一路"合作文件,成为意大利之后第二个加入"一带一路"的欧盟创始成员国。

通过"空中丝绸之路"建设,河南与卢森堡的合作领域在不断加强,"一带一路"经济合作论坛先后在郑州和卢森堡举办,形成双年交替举办机制;卢森堡金融推广署金融推介会在郑州举行,豫卢金融合作领域不断拓展;河南省博物院文物赴卢展出等活动相继举行,豫卢两地多元化的开放合作平台逐步建成。一系列的活动推动了双方高层领导人员互访,促进了两地人民之间的交流和文化互动,实现了经济效益与社会效益的"双赢合作"。

2. 卢森堡货航亚洲市场发展展望

由于国际贸易摩擦和全球经济增长放缓两重因素叠加,2019年的全球航空货运量自2012年以来首次下降,这也是自2008年金融危机以来,航空货运市场表现最差的一年,整个货运市场萎缩了9.7%,其中受冲击最大的当属亚太地区。

新冠肺炎疫情让2020年的航空货运市场的不确定性陡然上升,它的出现基本上扑灭了国际航空运输协会(IATA)对2020年全球货运市场"温和复苏"的预测。国际航空运输协会2020年3月份全球航空货运数据显示,全球航空货运需求同比去年下降15.2%(国际市场下降15.8%)、货运运力同比去年下降22.7%(国际市场下降24.6%)、国际航空货运运力与去年同期相比萎缩43.7%。

随着疫情在欧洲蔓延,英国、瑞典、德国等多家欧洲支线航空公司深陷破产重组危机;德国泰格尔机场宣布,从2020年6月15日起临时关闭两个月;挪威航空在经历了包括重大重组、股票发行和股价暴跌在内的几天之后,迎来了一系列新股东;德国政府表示将为汉莎航空提供90亿欧元的资助,法国政府同法国航空—荷兰皇家航空集团达成70亿欧元的援助计划。全球航空运输业成为遭受新冠肺炎疫情打击的重灾区。

been alternately held in Zhengzhou and Luxembourg. Luxembourg Financial Promotion Agency holds its conference in Zhengzhou, and financial cooperation between the two countries continues to expand. Activities such as the exhibition of cultural relics from Henan Museum have been held in Luxembourg, and a diverse range of open cooperation platforms have gradually been built. These activities have resulted in mutual visits between senior leaders, cultural exchanges between the people of both countries, as well as numerous economic and social benefits.

2. Prospects of Cargolux Airlines International in the Asian Market

Beset by international trade frictions and decelerated global economic growth, global air cargo volume declined in 2019 for the first time since 2012. It was also the worst year for the air cargo market since the 2008 financial crisis. The entire cargo market shrank by 9.7%, and the Asia-Pacific region suffered the most.

The COVID-19 outbreak has intensified the uncertainty in air freight markets, largely wiping out the International Air Transport Association's forecast of a "moderate recovery" in 2020. According to the International Air Transport Association's data for March 2020, global air cargo demand declined by 15.2% (international market down by 15.8%), freight capacity declined by 22.7% (international market down by 24.6%), and international air cargo capacity shrank by 43.7% compared with the corresponding period last year.

With the spread of the epidemic in Europe, many European regional airlines, such as those in the UK, Sweden and Germany, entered a bankruptcy and restructuring crisis. Tegel Airport in Germany announced that it would close for two months beginning on June 15, 2020. After major restructuring and a plunge in its share price, Norwegian Air Shuttle was taken over by new shareholders. The German Government said it would provide 9 billion euros in funding for Lufthansa Airlines, while the French Government and Air France-KLM Group agreed on an aid plan of 7 billion euros. The global air transport industry has been hard hit by the COVID-19 outbreak.

Henan is an important market for routes and operations of Cargolux Airlines International, and Zhenghzou is the largest hub of Cargolux Airlines International in China's mainland. In such an uncertain market environment,

河南是卢森堡货航航线和运营的重要市场，郑州是卢森堡货航在中国大陆的最大枢纽，过去是如此，未来亦将如此。在如此糟糕的市场环境下，卢森堡货航对未来的发展仍然持有信心。信心来源于以下三个方面。

第一，中欧之间良好的国际贸易发展趋势仍将持续。2018年，欧盟是中国第一大贸易合作伙伴，中欧双边贸易额同比增长7.9%；2019年，欧盟作为中国第二大贸易合作伙伴，中欧双边贸易额为4.86万亿元人民币，同比增长8%。卢森堡货航在中国市场拥有郑州、香港两个运输枢纽，2020年，中欧贸易可能因为新冠肺炎疫情因素面临下降压力，但长期而言，中欧贸易的良好发展趋势将为卢森堡货航带来重要的市场运营基础。

第二，在"一带一路"合作框架下，卢森堡货航可获中国政府支持，在中国开设更多通航点。2019年，卢森堡货航新增郑州—布达佩斯—卢森堡、郑州—厦门—洛杉矶洲际航线，米兰—郑州航线增加首尔为经停点。未来，卢森堡货航将继续通过加密航班、优化航线网络方式提升运营效能。

第三，在河南省政府的支持下，通过河南跨境贸易新需求带动企业发展。在河南省政府的领导下，郑州机场的跨境货物集散能力呈现良好的长期增长势头，已经成为中国跨境贸易货物重要空港之一。卢森堡货航作为郑州机场最大的国际航空货运供应商，将从中获益。

3. 积极参与河南航空经济建设，将双方合作推向更高水平

卢森堡处于欧洲心脏地带，辐射近5亿欧盟人口，是高度发达经济体，人均GDP连续多年排名世界第一。在世界三大评级机构的主权评级中，卢森堡评级均为最优。卢森堡政局稳定，法律健全，税收优惠，经济开放，重视自由贸易和保护投资。

河南省地处中国腹地，享有横贯东西、联结南北方的地利之便。

Cargolux Airlines International still has confidence in its future development. The confidence comes from the following three aspects.

First, the sound development trend of international trade between China and Europe continues. In 2018, the EU was China's largest trading partner, and bilateral trade volume between China and Europe has increased by 7.9% year-on-year. In 2019, the EU, China's second largest trading partner, had a bilateral trade volume of 4.86 trillion yuan, an 8% increase compared with the previous year. Cargolux Airlines International has two transportation hubs in the Chinese market: Zhengzhou and Hong Kong. In 2020, China-EU trade may face downward pressure due to the epidemic, but in the long run, the sound development of China-EU trade will be the foundation for Cargolux Airlines International's market operation.

Second, according to the cooperation agreement of the Belt and Road Initiative signed between Luxembourg and China, Cargolux Airlines International can get support from the Chinese Government and open more destinations in China. In 2019, Cargolux Airlines International added three intercontinental routes: Zhengzhou-Budapest-Luxembourg, Zhengzhou-Xiamen-Los Angeles, and Seoul-Zhengzhou-Milan. In the future, Cargolux Airlines International will continue to enhance its operational efficiency by increasing the number of flights and optimizing its route network.

Third, with the support of the Henan Provincial Government, the development of enterprises will be driven by the new demand of cross-border trade in Henan. Under the leadership of Henan Provincial Government, the Zhengzhou Airport Economic Zone has shown strong momentum of long-term growth in its cross-border cargo distribution capacity, and has become one of the most important airports for China's cross-border trade. Cargolux Airlines International will benefit from being the largest air cargo supplier to the Zhengzhou Airport Economic Zone.

3. Take an Active Part in Henan's Aviation Economic Construction to Promote Cooperation between Luxembourg and China

Luxembourg is in the heart of Europe, with a highly developed economy whose per capita GDP has ranked first in the world for many years. Among the

卢森堡货航已经成为郑州机场的国际货运龙头企业，卢森堡货航选择了河南，是看中了这里的未来。当地政府没有把一条航线仅仅当成一个交易，而是当作一个地区发展航空经济的突破口，河南计划通过20年的时间打造国际货运枢纽，让未来市场的发展前景充满信心。

郑州与卢森堡有很多相似之处，而且卢森堡货航也找到了河南航投这个非常敬业和信赖的合作伙伴，"双枢纽"战略模式可实现双方诉求，形成共赢的良性发展。

过去的时间，卢森堡货航见证了当初选择的正确性，更加坚定了在河南投资发展、实现合作共赢的信心。而且随着河南对外开放水平的不断提升，河南、郑州正在被越来越多的欧洲人所知晓，阔步登上世界的舞台。走进郑州航空港经济综合实验区，仿佛看到了河南"腾飞的翅膀"，今后，卢森堡货航还将进一步加密航线，不断拓展合作领域，努力把双方的合作推向新高度。

河南"空中丝绸之路"因合作而起步，因磨砺而宽阔。它正用不断进取的事实向世人表明，一群坚持互惠共赢的奋斗者以蓝天为背板奋力书写出时代新篇章，一条跨越万里山河的运输线以国际市场为乐谱奏出恢弘的时代新交响。画卷延绵，弦乐和唱。河南"空中丝绸之路"将拥有更加绚烂的未来！

sovereign ratings of the world's three foremost rating agencies, Luxembourg is in first place. Luxembourg has a stable political situation, sound laws, preferential taxation, and an open economy. It values free trade and investment protection.

Cargolux Airlines International has become the leading international cargo enterprise of Zhengzhou Airport. The reason why Cargolux Airlines International chose Henan lies in its ideal location. The local government does not regard a new trade route as just a transaction, but as a breakthrough in the development of the regional aviation economy. Henan plans to become an international freight hub within 20 years, and Cargolux Airlines International can be confident in the prospects of the markets here.

Cargolux Airlines International has found Henan Civil Aviation Development and Investment Co., Ltd. to be a dedicated and trusted partner. The "double hubs" strategic model can realize the demands of both parties and lead to win-win development.

In the past few years, Cargolux Airlines International has further strengthened its confidence in investing in Henan. With the increasing integration of Henan into the global market economy, Henan and Zhengzhou are moving onto the world stage. Upon entering Zhengzhou Airport, you can feel the "wings" of Henan Province. In the future, Cargolux Airlines International will continue to expand flights and routes, and strive to promote cooperation between the two parties.

The "Silk Road in the Air" in Henan started from cooperation and was broadened by hard work. It is using continuous progress to show the world that a group of fighters who insist on mutual benefit are working hard to write a new chapter of the era. A transportation line that spans thousands of miles of mountains and rivers is playing a new symphony of the era with the international market as the music score. The "Silk Road in the Air" in Henan will have a more splendid future!

附：河南"空中丝绸之路"大事记

2013年2月25日，河南民航发展投资有限公司（简称"河南航投"）与卢森堡政府开始接洽，表达收购卢森堡国际货运航空公司（简称"卢森堡货航"）35%股权的意向，并提出相关商业合作计划。

2013年3月13日，时任河南省省长郭庚茂与时任卢森堡可持续发展与基础产业部部长克劳德·维斯勒在北京举行了首次会谈，确定了合作意向和基本战略合作方向。

2013年4月8日，河南航投代表团赴卢森堡与对方商谈卢森堡货航股权收购及商业合作事宜，提出希望卢森堡航空企业、物流企业入驻郑州机场开展业务，建立郑州—卢森堡"双枢纽"，加强河南省与欧洲的经贸往来。

2013年6月23日，河南航投根据对方要求递交了第一阶段的竞标材料。

2013年7月12日，河南航投正式收到卢方通知，顺利进入第二轮竞标。

2013年9月13日，河南航投向卢方提交有法律约束力的收购要约。

2013年10月初，河南航投在第二轮竞标中胜出。

2013年11月28日，卢森堡政府宣布河南航投在并购竞标中胜出，同意出售卢森堡货航35%的股权。

2013年12月13日，卢森堡货航董事会批准了河南航投的收购方案。

2014年1月14日，河南航投收购卢森堡货航股权暨双方商业合作签约仪式在郑州举行。时任河南省省长谢伏瞻、时任副省长赵建才出席签约仪式。"郑州—卢森堡"双枢纽正式确立。

2014年4月23日，河南航投与卢森堡政府正式完成了卢森堡货航股权交割和商业登记变更。

Appendix: Milestones of the "Silk Road in the Air" in Henan Province

On February 25, 2013, Henan Civil Aviation Development and Investment Co., Ltd.(HNCA) contacted the Luxembourg Government, expressing its intention to acquire 35% of the shares of Cargolux Airlines International and proposing relevant business cooperation plans.

On March 13, 2013, Guo Gengmao, then Governor of Henan Province, and Claude Weissler, then Minister of the Ministry of Sustainable Development and Basic Industry of Luxembourg, held the first meeting in Beijing and confirmed the cooperative intention as well as the direction of basic strategy.

On April 8, 2013, the delegation of Henan Civil Aviation Development and Investment Co., Ltd. was sent to Luxembourg to negotiate share acquisition of Cargolux Airlines International and business cooperation with the Luxembourg Government. Their hope was for Luxembourg aviation and logistics enterprises to settle in Zhengzhou Airport, and to promote economic and trade ties between Henan and Europe through the construction of the Zhengzhou-Luxembourg "double hubs".

On June 23, 2013, Henan Civil Aviation Development and Investment Co., Ltd. submitted the materials for the first round of bidding according to the requirements of the Luxembourg Government.

On July 12, 2013, Henan Civil Aviation Development and Investment Co., Ltd. received official notification from the Luxembourg Government and entered the second round of bidding smoothly.

On September 13, 2013, Henan Civil Aviation Development and Investment Co., Ltd. submitted a legally binding takeover offer to the Luxembourg Government.

In early October 2013, Henan Civil Aviation Development and Investment Co., Ltd. won the bid in the second round.

On November 28, 2013, the Luxembourg Government announced that Henan Civil Aviation Development and Investment Co., Ltd. won the merger bid and agreed to sell 35% of the shares of Cargolux Airlines International.

附：河南"空中丝绸之路"大事记

2014年6月27日，郑州至卢森堡国际货运航线开通仪式在郑州新郑国际机场举行。

2014年11月23日，河南航投在郑州机场举行了"郑州—卢森堡"航线超万吨仪式，庆祝卢森堡货航在5个月内货运总量超万吨。

2015年1月6日，卢森堡首相格扎维埃·贝泰尔接受新华社记者采访时表示，卢森堡货航与河南航投开展合作取得的丰硕成果表明，中国"丝绸之路经济带"和"21世纪海上丝绸之路"战略构想为中国和世界创造了共赢机遇。

2015年1月21日，时任中国民用航空局局长李家祥与卢森堡可持续

On December 13, 2013, the board of directors of Cargolux Airlines International approved the acquisition plan of Henan Civil Aviation Development and Investment Co., Ltd.

On January 14, 2014, Henan Civil Aviation Development and Investment Co., Ltd. and Cargolux Airlines International held the signing ceremony for share acquisition and bilateral business cooperation in Zhengzhou. Xie Fuzhan, then Governor of Henan Province, and Zhao Jiancai, then Vice Governor of Henan Province attended the ceremony. The Zhengzhou-Luxembourg "double hubs" was formally established.

On April 23, 2014, Henan Civil Aviation Development and Investment Co., Ltd. and the Luxembourg Government formally completed the equity delivery and changing procedures of business registration of Cargolux Airlines International.

On June 27, 2014, the opening ceremony of the International Freight Route between Zhengzhou and Luxembourg was held at Zhengzhou Xinzheng International Airport.

On November 23, 2014, Henan Civil Aviation Development and Investment Co., Ltd. held a ceremony to celebrate the total freight volume of Cargolux Airlines International on the Zhengzhou-Luxembourg route exceeding 10,000 tons within five months.

On January 6, 2015, Xavier Bettel, the Prime Minister of Luxembourg, said in an interview with Xinhua News Agency that fruitful achievements gained by the cooperation between Cargolux Airlines International and Henan Civil Aviation Development and Investment Co., Ltd. showed that the Chinese strategic initiatives, the Silk Road Economic Belt and the 21st Century Maritime Silk Road, created win-win opportunities for China and the whole world.

On January 21, 2015, Li Jiaxiang, then Director of the Civil Aviation Administration of China, and Francois Bosch, Minister of the Ministry of Sustainable Development and Basic Industry of Luxembourg signed a memorandum of understanding on aviation transport cooperation in Beijing.

On January 22, 2015, Henan Civil Aviation Development and Investment Co., Ltd. and Cargolux Airlines International signed a memorandum of cooperation in Zhengzhou. The two parties agreed to speed up the cooperation

发展与基础产业部部长弗朗索瓦·鲍施在京签署航空运输合作谅解备忘录。

2015年1月22日,河南航投与卢森堡货航在郑州签署了合作备忘录,双方同意将根据备忘录的内容,加快合作进程,推进各项目的逐级落地,为提升中—卢两国经济发展注入新动力。时任河南省省长谢伏瞻、时任副省长赵建才、卢森堡可持续发展与基础产业部部长弗朗索瓦·鲍施出席签约仪式。

2015年1月23日,河南航投跨境E贸易暨"新鲜卢森堡"项目启动仪式在郑州航空港经济综合实验区举行。该项目的启动标志着河南航投与卢森堡货航的合作扩展至国际贸易领域,双方合作从空中丝路向买卖全球迈进。时任河南省副省长赵建才、卢森堡可持续发展与基础产业部部长弗朗索瓦·鲍施出席仪式并致辞。

2015年5月18日,卢森堡货航"郑州号"正式开通"卢森堡—郑州—芝加哥"国际货运航线。此航线是郑州第一条采用第五航权的国际货运航线,标志着郑州成为中国重要的航空节点。

2015年6月19日,河南航投与卢森堡货航就在郑州成立中国合资货运航空公司、郑州合资飞机维修公司签署合作协议。

2015年10月18日,卢森堡货航在郑州召开成立2015年全球经理人大会。

2015年10月20日,卢森堡货航在郑州新郑国际机场举行45周年庆典仪式。卢森堡货航"米兰—郑州"航线加密至每周2班,卢森堡货航在郑州新郑国际机场的运力升至每周13班。

2015年11月23日,卢森堡货航在11个月内运送5.5万吨,提前超额完成全年目标,累计国际货运量、国际货运航线数、航班数量、国际通航点等主要指标跃居郑州新郑国际机场首位。

2015年12月18日,河南省首家保税展示交易单位在河南航投双向跨境E贸易进口商品展销中心揭牌。

according to the contents of the memorandum and push the implementation of each project step by step, so as to provide new impetus for the economic development of China and Luxembourg. Xie Fuzhan, then Governor of Henan Province, Zhao Jiancai, then Vice Governor of Henan Province, and Francois Bosch, Minister of the Ministry of Sustainable Development and Basic Industry of Luxembourg attended the signing ceremony.

On January 23, 2015, the launch ceremony of Cross-border E-trade and the "Fresh Luxembourg" Project was held in the Zhengzhou Airport Economy Zone, which marked the expansion of the cooperation between Henan Civil Aviation Development and Investment Co., Ltd. and Cargolux Airlines International into the field of international trade and bilateral cooperation. Zhao Jiancai, then Vice Governor of Henan Province, and Francois Bosch, Minister of the Ministry of Sustainable Development and Basic Industry of Luxembourg attended the ceremony and delivered speeches.

On May 18, 2015, Cargolux Airlines International officially opened the Luxembourg-Zhengzhou-Chicago freight route with the cargo aircraft named "Zhengzhou". This route is the first international freight route that adopts the Fifth Freedom rights in Zhengzhou, meaning that Zhengzhou has become an important aviation hub in China.

On June 19, 2015, Henan Civil Aviation Development and Investment Co., Ltd. signed a cooperation agreement with Cargolux Airlines International on setting up a cargo airline joint venture and an aircraft maintenance company in Zhengzhou.

On October 18, 2015, Cargolux Airlines International held the 2015 global managers' conference in Zhengzhou.

On October 20, 2015, Cargolux Airlines International held its 45th anniversary ceremony at Zhengzhou Xinzheng International Airport. Its Milan-Zhengzhou route was increased to 2 flights per week and the transport capacity at Zhengzhou Xinzheng International Airport rose to 13 flights a week.

On November 23, 2015, Cargolux Airlines International had transported 55,000 tons of cargoes within 11 months, exceeding the annual target ahead of schedule. Cargolux Airlines International ranked first in accumulative international freight volume, number of international freight routes, number of

2016年1月5日,河南航投与立陶宛AviaAM租赁集团开展融资租赁项目合作会谈,签署战略合作协议。

2016年5月24日,河南航投与立陶宛AviaAM租赁集团在郑州签署合资合同。双方约定,在郑州成立中外合资融资租赁公司,主要在飞机、航材设备及基础设施建设等领域开展业务合作。

2016年6月21日—24日,河南省政府及经贸考察团赴立陶宛进行友好访问,实地考察立陶宛AviaAM租赁集团、Avia 解决方案集团的飞机维修基地、飞行员培训学校和航空旅游项目。

2016年10月14日,时任卢森堡大公国驻华大使石泰嵋访问河南航投,表示卢森堡方面就开通郑州至卢森堡客运航线、设立飞行领事等问题与中国政府的相关部门进行沟通,并获得积极的回应,希望能够寻找恰当的时机,开展郑州与卢森堡之间的客运业务。

2017年2月28日,广东龙浩航空集团有限公司与河南航投磋商战略合作。

2017年6月12日,河南航投与卢森堡货航在北京正式签署合资合同,双方合资成立以郑州为基地的本土货运航空公司。中共中央政治局常委、国务院总理李克强与卢森堡首相格扎维埃·贝泰尔共同鉴证签约。

2017年6月13日,河南航投与时任卢森堡驻华大使石泰嵋签署《关于在河南开展签证便利业务谅解备忘录》。时任河南省委书记、省人大常委会主任谢伏瞻在郑州会见卢森堡首相格扎维埃·贝泰尔一行,并和时任省长陈润儿共同鉴证有关合作签约。

2017年6月14日,中国国家主席习近平在人民大会堂会见卢森堡首相贝泰尔。习近平指出,要深化双方在"一带一路"建设框架内金融和产能等合作,中方支持建设郑州—卢森堡"空中丝绸之路";要加强文化、教育、体育等人文交流,提高人员往来便利化水平;中方期待卢方在中欧关系中继续发挥积极作用,推动欧盟为中欧合作深入发展提供更

flights, and number of international navigation destinations.

On December 18, 2015, the first bonded exhibition and trading institution of Henan Province was unveiled in the Import Commodities Exhibition and Sales Center of two-way cross-border E-trade of Henan Civil Avistion Development and Investment Co. Ltd..

On January 5, 2016, Henan Civil Aviation Development and Investment Co., Ltd. and Lithuania AviaAM Leasing Group held talks on the cooperation of financial leasing and signed a strategic cooperation agreement.

On May 24, 2016, Henan Civil Aviation Development and Investment Co., Ltd. and Lithuania AviaAM Leasing Group signed a joint venture contract in Zhengzhou. It was agreed that a Sino-foreign financial leasing joint venture would be established in Zhengzhou. The two parties are mainly engaged in business cooperation in the fields of aircraft, aeronautical material and equipment as well as infrastructure construction.

From June 21-24, 2016, Henan's Provincial Government and economic and trade delegation paid a friendly visit to Lithuania, and toured the aircraft maintenance base, pilot training school and air travel projects of Lithuania AviaAM Leasing Group and Avia Solutions Group.

On October 14, 2016, Luxembourg's then-Ambassador to China visited Henan Civil Aviation Development and Investment Co., Ltd.. He confirmed that the Luxembourg Government had communicated with relevant departments of the Chinese Government on issues such as opening a passenger flight route from Zhengzhou to Luxembourg and setting up the flight consular, and that he hoped to find the right moment to start passenger transport between Zhengzhou and Luxembourg.

On February 28, 2017, Guangdong Longhao Airlines Group Co., Ltd. and Henan Civil Aviation Development and Investment Co., Ltd. discussed strategic cooperation.

On June 12, 2017, Henan Civil Aviation Development and Investment Co., Ltd. and Cargolux Airlines International formally signed a joint venture contract in Beijing to establish a local cargo airline based in Zhengzhou. Li Keqiang, Member of the Standing Committee of the Political Bureau of the CPC Central Committee and Premier of the State Council, signed the agreement with Xavier

多有利条件。

2017年7月28日，中信旅游集团与河南航投磋商开通郑—卢客运包机及欧盟签证便利化等相关业务合作。

2017年8月11日至15日，河南省政府出访团访问波兰、卢森堡，与罗兹机场、彩虹旅行社签署关于机场建设和航线开通及旅游包机业务的合作备忘录；与卢布林机场、卢森堡商会分别签署合作备忘录；与卢森堡货航、卢森堡航空公司分别签订合作备忘录、合作协议等文件。

2017年8月17日，河南省政府常务会议讨论研究推进郑州—卢森堡"空中丝绸之路"建设等工作，提出要将"空中丝路"打造成为引领中部、服务全国、联通欧亚、辐射世界的空中经济廊道，推动河南实现更高水平对外开放，在支撑"一带一路"建设和服务全国大局中发挥更大作用。

2017年8月21日，河南省委常委会召开会议，贯彻落实习近平总书记支持建设郑州—卢森堡"空中丝绸之路"重要指示精神，研究河南省推进郑州—卢森堡"空中丝绸之路"建设专项规划和工作方案。

2017年8月23日，由河南航投、中航信托股份有限公司、河南省现代服务业产业投资基金共同发起设立的中原丝路基金举行成立暨项目签约仪式，三方机构共同签署意向合作协议。

2017年9月13日，河南—卢森堡"一带一路"经济合作论坛在郑州举行。河南贸促会与卢森堡大公国商会签署合作谅解备忘录。河南航投与卢森堡商会签署合作备忘录，双方同意将"河南—卢森堡'一带一路'经济合作论坛"发展为定期机制，以双年交替形式举办，为中卢双方及其他"一带一路"沿线国家搭建互利互惠的新平台，并根据企业需要逐步拓宽论坛覆盖范围，适时举行金融推介会、电子商务推介会、旅游文化推介会等。

2017年9月27日，河南航投与立陶宛BAA航空培训学院签署战略合作协议，双方将在郑州设立及发展飞行员培训中心达成共识。该飞行员

Bettel, Prime Minister of Luxembourg.

On June 13, 2017, Henan Civil Aviation Development and Investment Co., Ltd. signed *The Memorandum of Understanding on Visa Facilitation Services in Henan Province* with Luxembourg's then-Ambassador to China. Xie Fuzhan, then-Secretary of the CPC Henan Provincial Committee and Director of the Standing Committee of Henan Provincial People's Congress, met with Luxembourg Prime Minister Xavier Bettel and his entourage in Zhengzhou. They and Chen Runer, the then-Governor of Henan Province, attended the signing of the cooperation.

On June 14, 2017, Chinese President Xi Jinping met with Xavier Bettel, Prime Minister of Luxembourg, at the Great Hall of the People. Xi called for deepening bilateral cooperation on finance and production capacity within the framework of the Belt and Road Initiative, and said China supported the construction of the "Silk Road in the Air" between Zhengzhou and Luxembourg. He suggested strengthening cultural, educational and sporting exchanges and facilitating personnel exchanges. He also said that China expects Luxembourg to continue to play a positive role in China-EU ties and push the EU to provide more favorable conditions for the in-depth development of China-EU cooperation.

On July 28, 2017, CITIC Tourism Group and Henan Civil Aviation Development and Investment Co., Ltd. discussed the launch of the Zhengzhou-Luxembourg passenger charter flight and EU visa facilitation, as well as other related business ventures.

From August 11 to 15, 2017, the delegation of Henan Provincial Government visited Poland and Luxembourg, and signed the memorandum of cooperation on airport construction, airline opening and tourism charter services with Rhodes Airport and Rainbow Travel Agency, the memorandum of cooperation with Lublin Airport and Luxembourg Chamber of Commerce, and the memorandum of cooperation, as well as other documents, with Cargolux Airlines International and Luxair Luxembourg Airlines.

On August 17, 2017, the Henan Provincial Government Executive Meeting discussed and studied how to promote the construction of the "Silk Road in the Air" between Zhengzhou and Luxembourg, and proposed making the "Silk

培训中心拟建设全能飞行模拟器的飞行员培训中心、机组成员培训中心，设置私人飞机执照和商业飞行员执照考取服务，开设ATPL航线运输飞行员执照培训综合课程等。

2018年3月4日，"空中丝绸之路"理论与实践研讨会在河南郑州召开。

2018年4月16日，卢森堡旅游签证（郑州）便捷服务平台在郑东新区龙湖举行揭牌仪式，郑州成为除北京、上海之外，国内第三个能够办理卢森堡签证的城市，实现河南办理签证业务零的突破。

2018年4月17日，2018中—卢（郑州—卢森堡）"空中丝绸之路"经贸合作高峰会在郑州举行。

2018年6月27日，河南卢森堡中心在郑州市郑东新区开工建设。项目建成后将成为河南"空中丝路"融入国家"一带一路"建设的"国际客厅"，提供"一站式"的涉外服务。

2018年7月9日，河南航投与卢森堡芬德尔国际机场在卢森堡首相府签署《关于开通郑州至卢森堡国际客运航线的合作意向书》。该项目将进一步推进豫卢人文交流，为豫欧民心相通蓄势增能。河南省委书记王国生、卢森堡首相贝泰尔出席签约仪式。

2018年7月10日，河南省代表团在卢森堡参访卢森堡货航，调研河南航投与卢森堡货航合作情况。

2018年9月17日，卢森堡货航2018年第五次董事会会议在郑州召开，推动落实了郑州—卢森堡"空中丝绸之路"及"双枢纽"发展战略，合资货运航空公司开通、运营郑州—卢森堡客运航线等重点项目落地。

2018年11月7日，"华夏文明之源——河南文物珍宝展"文物启航仪式在郑州航空港万怡酒店举行，145件（组）精选文物精品由卢森堡货航专业货机运赴卢森堡。

2018年11月14日，卢森堡金融推介会在郑州举行。此次会议是卢森

Road in the Air" an economic corridor which can lead the central region, serve the country, connect Europe and Asia, and radiate the world, thereby motivating Henan to achieve a higher level of opening to the outside world, and play a greater role in the construction of the Belt and Road Initiative and serving the whole country.

On August 21, 2017, the Standing Committee of Henan Provincial Party Committee held a meeting to implement General Secretary Xi Jinping's guidelines for the construction of the "Silk Road in the Air" between Zhengzhou and Luxembourg, and to design specialized plannings and work programs of Henan Province for promoting the construction of the "Silk Road in the Air" between Zhengzhou and Luxembourg.

On August 23, 2017, the ceremony was held for the establishment and signing of the Zhongyuan Silk Road Fund, co-founded by Henan Civil Aviation Development and Investment Co., Ltd., Avic Trust Co., Ltd. and Henan Modern Service Industry Investment Fund, with the three parties signing a letter of intent for cooperation.

On September 13, 2017, the Henan-Luxembourg Belt and Road Initiative Economic Cooperation Forum was held in Zhengzhou. The Airlines Council for the Promotion of International Trade and the Luxembourg Chamber of Commerce signed a memorandum of understanding on cooperation. Henan Civil Aviation Development and Investment Co., Ltd. and the Luxembourg Chamber of Commerce signed a memorandum of cooperation. The two parties agreed to hold a Henan-Luxembourg Belt and Road Initiative Economic Cooperation Forum every two years, in order to build a mutually beneficial platform for China, Luxembourg and other countries along the Belt and Road, and gradually broaden the coverage of the forum to incorporate finance, electronic business, tourist culture, etc..

On September 27, 2017, Henan Civil Aviation Development and Investment Co., Ltd. and Lithuania BAA Aviation Training Institute signed a strategic cooperation agreement, and the two parties reached a consensus on the establishment and development of a pilot training center in Zhengzhou. The center planed to build a pilot training center and a crew member training center for the all-around flight simulator, set up private aircraft license and commercial

堡首次在京沪之外的中国大陆城市召开，表明河南"空中丝绸之路"在资金融通方面取得新进展。

2019年2月28日，河南航投与港中旅华贸国际物流股份有限公司在上海签约成立河南航投物流（卢森堡）有限责任公司。

2019年3月14日，由外交部国际经济司支持，国家发展改革委"一带一路"建设促进中心主办的"一带一路"国际合作典型项目研讨会在郑州开幕。郑州—卢森堡"空中丝绸之路"被誉为"一带一路"国际合作的生动实践。

pilot license examination services, and offer comprehensive courses for ATPL airline transport pilot license training.

On March 4, 2018, a seminar on the theory and practice of the "Silk Road in the Air" was held in Zhengzhou, Henan Province.

On April 16, 2018, the Luxembourg Tourist Visa (Zhengzhou) Convenient Service Platform was inaugurated in Longhu Lake, Zhengdong New District, making Zhengzhou the third city in China to enable people to apply for a Luxembourg visa, in addition to Beijing and Shanghai.

On April 17, 2018, the 2018 China-Luxembourg "Silk Road in the Air" Economic and Trade Cooperation Summit was held in Zhengzhou.

On June 27, 2018, the construction of the Henan Luxemburg Center began in Zhengdong New District. Once completed, it will become the "international living room" for the "Silk Road in the Air" in Henan Province, and provide "one-stop" foreign-related services.

On July 9, 2018, Henan Civil Aviation Development and Investment Co., Ltd. and Luxembourg Findel Airport signed *The Letter of Intent for Cooperation on Opening International Passenger Flight Routes between Zhengzhou and Luxembourg* at the Prime Minister's Office of Luxembourg. The project further promoted cultural exchanges between Henan and Luxembourg, and closer ties between Henan and Europe. Wang Guosheng, then-Secretary of the CPC Henan Provincial Committee and Xavier Bettel, the Prime Minister of Luxembourg, attended the signing ceremony.

On July 10, 2018, a delegation from Henan Province visited Cargolux Airlines International in Luxembourg to investigate the cooperation between Henan Civil Aviation Development and Investment Co., Ltd. and Cargolux Airlines International.

On September 17, 2018, the fifth board meeting of Cargolux Airlines International in 2018 was held in Zhengzhou, promoting the development of the "Silk Road in the Air" and "double hubs" between Zhengzhou and Luxembourg, the cargo airline joint venture, the opening of Zhengzhou-Luxembourg passenger flight routes and other key projects.

On November 7, 2018, "Origin of Chinese Civilization: Exhibition of Cultural Heritage Treasures in Henan" was held at the Courtyard by Marriott in

2019年3月28日,布达佩斯机场与河南航投签署谅解备忘录,将进一步扩大国际航空货运市场并提升布达佩斯机场及郑州新郑国际机场在航空运输业的地位。

2019年4月3日,卢森堡货航正式开通卢森堡—布达佩斯—郑州国际货运航线,每周两班。此航线的开通完善了卢森堡货航在郑州货运航线网络建设,织密了河南"空中丝绸之路"。

2019年6月14日,河南省首家本土基地货运航空公司——中原龙浩航空有限公司正式揭牌运营。中原龙浩航空有限公司将以郑州新郑国际机场和广州白云国际机场进行"双基地"运营,通过"国内+洲际"运输模式实现航线、航权等多方面互补,推动郑州—卢森堡"双枢纽"战略高质量发展。

2019年6月24日,中原龙浩航空有限公司首次完成柬埔寨金边国际机场至海口美兰国际机场活体动物包机运输任务。

2019年7月1日,卢森堡—郑州—厦门—洛杉矶货运航线正式开通。这是河南"空中丝绸之路"开辟的又一条第五航权航线。洛杉矶成为继芝加哥、亚特兰大之后,卢森堡货航在北美市场的又一重要通航点。

2019年7月5日,中原龙浩航空有限公司广州—武汉航线首航成功。该航线是中原龙浩航空有限公司开通的第20条货运航线。

2019年10月25日,BAA(中国)航空培训中心项目建设动员大会在郑州航空港经济综合实验区举行,中原首家航空培训中心正式开工建设。

2019年11月4日,河南—卢森堡"一带一路"经济合作论坛在郑州举行。与会企业代表与专家分享郑州—卢森堡"双枢纽"合作经验与成果,探索未来互利共赢新机遇。

2020年1月10日,在河南省第十三届人民代表大会第三次会议上,时任河南省省长尹弘指出支持开展郑州—卢森堡"空中丝绸之路"运邮业务。

Zhengzhou Airport Economy Zone. 145 selected artifacts were transported to Luxembourg by a dedicated cargo plane of Cargolux Airlines International.

On November 14, 2018, the Luxembourg Financial Promotion Conference was held in Zhengzhou. It was the first time that the meeting had been held in a city in the mainland of China except Beijing and Shanghai, indicating new progress in the financing of the "Silk Road in the Air" in Henan Province.

On February 28, 2019, Henan Civil Aviation Development and Investment Co., Ltd. and CTS International Logistics Corporation Limited signed a contract to establish HNCA Logistics (Luxemburg) Co., Ltd. in Shanghai.

On March 14, 2019, the Seminar on International Cooperation Projects of the Belt and Road Initiative opened in Zhengzhou. It was supported by the Department of International Economic Affairs of the Ministry of Foreign Affairs. The "Silk Road in the Air" between Zhengzhou and Luxemburg was hailed as a vivid example of international cooperation on the Belt and Road Initiative.

On March 28, 2019, Budapest Airport and Henan Civil Aviation Development and Investment Co., Ltd. signed a memorandum of understanding, which expanded the international air cargo market and enhanced the position of Budapest Airport and Zhengzhou Xinzheng International Airport in the air transport industry.

On April 3, 2019, Cargolux Airlines International officially opened the Luxembourg-Budapest-Zhengzhou international freight route, with two flights per week, widening the freight route network of Cargolux Airlines International in Zhengzhou and expanding the "Silk Road in the Air" in Henan Province.

On June 14, 2019, Longhao Airlines Co., Ltd., the first cargo airline based in Henan Province, was officially inaugurated. It is operated by the "double bases" of Zhengzhou Xinzheng International Airport and Guangzhou Baiyun International Airport and balances domestic and international transportation, thereby promoting the high-quality development of the "Silk Road in the Air".

On June 24, 2019, Longhao Airlines Co., Ltd. completed the first charter flight of living animals from Phnom Penh International Airport in Cambodia to Haikou Meilan International Airport.

On July 1, 2019, the Luxemburg-Zhengzhou-Xiamen-Los Angeles freight route was officially opened, adopting the Fifth Freedom Rights, and adding

附：河南"空中丝绸之路"大事记

2020年3月22日，首批河南省委省政府为卢森堡紧急筹措的医疗物资，由卢森堡货航运送至卢森堡，郑州—卢森堡"空中丝绸之路"成为全球抗疫背景下的友谊之路。

2020年6月9日，中原龙浩开通广州—郑州—首尔"双基地"国际货运航线，打通了以郑州为中心、纵贯华南和东北亚市场的南北空中经济廊道，进一步增强了郑州中心枢纽的集疏能力，同时也为卢森堡货航在郑州实现"空空中转"奠定了基础。

2020年6月14日，BAA（中国）航空培训中心启动，民航局为其颁证。

another important navigation point for Cargolux Airlines International in the North American market.

On July 5, 2019, China Central Longhao Airlines Co., Ltd. successfully completed the first flight of the route between Guangzhou and Wuhan, which was the 20th freight route opened by the airline.

On October 25, 2019, a promotional event for the construction of the BAA (China) Aviation Training Center was held in the Zhengzhou Airport Economy Zone, and construction of the first aviation training center in central China officially started.

On November 4, 2019, the Henan-Luxembourg Belt and Road Initiative Economic Cooperation Forum was held in Zhengzhou. Business representatives and experts shared experiences and achievements of "double hubs" cooperation between Zhengzhou and Luxembourg, and explored new opportunities for mutual benefit in the future.

On January 10, 2020, at the third meeting of the 13th People's Congress of Henan Province, Yin Hong, then Governor of Henan Province, pointed out that he supports the development of Zhengzhou-Luxembourg "Silk Road in the Air" postal services.

On March 22, 2020, the first batch of medical supplies urgently raised by Henan Provincial Government for Luxembourg were transported by Cargolux Airlines International to Luxembourg. Zhengzhou-Luxembourg "Silk Road in the Air" became a road of friendship in the context of the global fight against the epidemic.

On June 9, 2020, Longhao Airlines opened the Guangzhou-Zhengzhou-Seoul "dual-base" international freight route, which serves as a north-south air economic corridor with Zhengzhou as the center and runs through the markets of South China and Northeast Asia. This freight route further strengthened Zhengzhou's ability as a hub to collect and distribute cargoes, and also laid the foundation for Cargolux Airlines International's "air-to-air transshipment" in Zhengzhou.

On June 14, 2020, the BAA (China) Aviation Training Center was launched, and the Civil Aviation Administration issued a certificate for it.

On September 8, 2020, the second "Silk Road in the Air" Cooperation

2020年9月8日，第二届"空中丝绸之路"合作峰会在中国国际服务贸易会期间举办，郑州—卢森堡"空中丝绸之路"作为民航支撑引领地方经济高质量发展的"河南样板"，在峰会上被作为专题研讨。

2020年9月8日，在第二届"空中丝绸之路"国际合作峰会上，河南航投分别与航空工业通飞、法国Simaero公司、中检集团、京东集团等签署战略合作协议。

Summit was held during China International Service Trade Conference. At the summit, the Zhengzhou-Luxembourg "Silk Road in the Air" was discussed as a "Henan model" with which civil aviation supports and leads the high-quality development of the local economy.

On September 8, 2020, at the second "Silk Road in the Air" International Cooperation Summit, Henan Civil Aviation Development and Investment Co., Ltd. signed strategic cooperation agreements with China Aviation Industry General Aircraft Co., Ltd., France Simaero, China Certification and Inspection (Group) Co., Ltd., JD.com and others.